DAVID VEALE, FRCPsych, MD, BSc, MPhil, Dip CACP is a consultant psychiatrist in Cognitive Behavior Therapy at the South London and Maudsley NHS Foundation Trust and the Priory Hospital, North London. He is an Honorary Senior Lecturer at the Institute of Psychiatry, King's College London. He is an accredited cognitive behavior therapist and President of the British Association of Behavioural and Cognitive Psychotherapies 2006–8. He has about 50 publications to his name, accessible through his website www.veale.co.uk. He has been helping people with depression and anxiety disorders for more than 15 years.

ROB WILLSON, BSc, MSc, Dip SBHS is a cognitive behavior therapist in private practice. He also works as a tutor at Goldsmiths College, University of London. He holds an honours degree in Psychology, an MSc in Rational Emotive Behaviour Therapy, and a Postgraduate Diploma in Social and Behavioural Health Studies. He has been involved in treating people with depression and anxiety for the past 12 years.

David Veale and Rob Willson are authors of *Overcoming Obsessive Compulsive Disorder*, also published by Robinson.

Other titles in the *Overcoming* series:

3-part self-help courses

Overcoming Anxiety Self-Help Course
Overcoming Bulimia Nervosa and Binge-Eating Self-Help Course
Overcoming Low Self-Esteem Self-Help Course
Overcoming Panic and Agoraphobia Self-Help Course
Overcoming Social Anxiety and Shyness Self-Help Course

Single-volume books

Overcoming Anger and Irritability
Overcoming Anorexia Nervosa
Overcoming Anxiety
Bulimia Nervosa and Binge-Eating
Overcoming Childhood Trauma
Overcoming Chronic Fatigue
Overcoming Chronic Pain
Overcoming Compulsive Gambling
Overcoming Depression
Overcoming Insomnia and Sleep Problems
Overcoming Low Self-Esteem
Overcoming Mood Swings
Overcoming Obsessive Compulsive Disorder
Overcoming Panic
Overcoming Paranoid and Suspicious Thoughts
Overcoming Problem Drinking
Overcoming Relationship Problems
Overcoming Sexual Problems
Overcoming Social Anxiety and Shyness
Overcoming Traumatic Stress
Overcoming Weight Problems
Overcoming Your Child's Fears and Worries
Overcoming Your Smoking Habit

MANAGE YOUR MOOD

How to use Behavioral Activation techniques to overcome depression

David Veale and Rob Willson

ROBINSON
London

ROBINSON

First published in Great Britain in 2007 by Robinson

5 7 9 10 8 6 4

Copyright © David Veale and Rob Willson, 2007

'Your Fitness Personality Profile' (p.147) and 'Fitness Personality Profile' (p.148)
copyright © 2005, James Gavin PhD and taken from *Lifestyle Fitness Coaching*,
Human Kinetics Europe Ltd, 2005

The moral right of the authors has been asserted.

Important Note
This book is not intended as a substitute for medical advice or treatment.
Any person with a condition requiring medical attention should consult a
qualified medical practitioner or suitable therapist.

A CIP catalogue record for this book
is available from the British Library.

ISBN: 978-1-84529-314-7

Printed and bound in Great Britain by Ashford Colour Press

Robinson
An imprint of
Little, Brown Book Group
Carmelite House
50 Victoria Embankment
London EC4Y 0DZ

An Hachette UK Company
www.hachette.co.uk

www.improvementzone.co.uk

Contents

Note for practitioners

If you are using this book with your client you should be aware that it is based on Behavioral Activation (BA) which is part of the family of Behavioral and Cognitive Psychotherapies and derived from the treatment manual, *Depression in Context: Strategies for Guided Action* by Martell et al (2001) (see Appendix 4.) There are differences between the standard activity scheduling of cognitive behavior therapy (CBT) and that of BA. BA is rooted in a contextual functional analysis of activities that are being avoided, or that have the function of avoidance (e.g. ruminating). This information then guides the choices in the activity scheduling. The aim is to help people develop a pattern of approach behaviors rather than avoidance. We have added elements of Acceptance and Commitment Therapy (ACT) by also encouraging activities that are in keeping with one's valued directions in life. The distinctive feature of BA, ACT and newer approaches in CBT is the *process* of thinking (e.g. rumination, worry, self-attacking) rather than trying to change the *content* of a person's thoughts. Thought records and identifying schemas and assumptions are therefore not used unless, for example, it is to identify and determine the helpfulness of one's assumptions about ruminating or self-attacking. This book can be used in guided self-help for stepped care for mild to moderate depression, which in the future we hope to evaluate.

David Veale and Rob Willson

Foreword

Depression is a very common problem in the world today – and the number of reported cases is rising. It is estimated that 1 in 4 women and 1 in 7 men will have an episode of depression at some point in their lives, with many episodes beginning in early childhood and adolescence. Research has shown that in some communities, particularly the impoverished, depression can be even more widespread.

One of the difficulties with understanding depression is that it can vary depending upon the individual. Some people experience high levels of anxiety and a sense of dread; others experience elevated anger, frustration and irritability. Some eat more while others eat less. Most people suffering from depression have difficulty sleeping, but again, this can vary enormously from case to case. Despite these variations there are commonalities. For many, depression is seen as a state of exhaustion – you can feel physically, mentally and socially exhausted. This exhaustion can drain away positive feelings and interest in others and your environment. The combination of feelings of dread and fatigue, plus a negative outlook can make you want to hide away.

Over the centuries there have been many treatments for depression. More recent treatments include medications and specific psychological interventions. It is well known that depressed people's negative thinking and predictions about others and their environment make them more likely to give up and thus spiral downwards into depression. Research was conducted to explore whether helping people directly to change their thinking, behavior and level of activities could be helpful. The answer was it definitely could. For instance, regular exercise can really help to combat depression. By gradually increasing your level of activity, focusing on small but important steps, you can start to reduce the effects of depression.

David Veale and Rob Willson have written *Manage Your Mood* to share with you some of the ways you can understand your thinking style and reorganize your daily routines and activities to help overcome your depression. By doing this you can start to take control of your life rather than battling on as before, simply keeping going, or just putting on a brave face.

Many of the ideas outlined in *Manage Your Mood* are derived from what are called behavioral approaches to problems. This works on the basic idea that in order for us to learn new tasks or overcome difficulties and anxieties *skilful action* is required, for example, if we are anxious about learning to drive, the best way to develop our skill and confidence is to get in a car and practise with an instructor. Think of how many difficulties you have overcome in life by actually going out and tackling your problem – even when anxious!

When it comes to depression, *skilful action* means:

1 Recognizing what was happening in your life that triggered depression. Sometimes it can be a life event such as the break-up of a relationship, or a combination of difficulties that just seemed to happen simultaneously. Some degree of depression may be a natural way we deal with things when we feel over loaded.

2 Noting the way a life event elicited certain, understandable but unhelpful, coping efforts and behaviors in you as you tried to adapt to the context and stressor. This will show you how depression is now piloting your life.

3 Recognizing how those behaviors (called 'secondary problems' such as avoidance and rumination) can themselves become sources of depression. For example, when feeling low you might start to avoid activities or people. Think back to the driving example. This does not mean that simply increasing activities is always the answer; much depends on how helpful you find the activities.

In *Manage Your Mood*, David Veale and Rob Willson outline which behaviors can make your depression unintentionally worse and what actions can be used to help. For example, hiding in bed and ruminating – while sometimes an understandable reaction – can allow the depression to deepen and 'settle in', making you feel much worse. In contrast, encouraging yourself to get up and do one or two things during the day can help a little and boost your confidence.

This book also contains strategies to help you develop plans to take on your depression, while factoring in the fatigue inherent in depression. Above all, David Veale and Rob Willson provide invaluable advice on how to be kind to yourself in order to get better. *Manage Your Mood* is not intended as an instant 'cure' for depression but instead provides a wealth of strategies for working with depression to overcome it and achieve your life goals. Written by two authors with many years of clinical experience and research, *Manage Your Mood* is necessary reading for anyone struggling to cope with depression.

Professor Paul Gilbert,
Professor of Clinical Psychology at the University of Derby and Head of
Specialty, Adult Mental Health for the Derbyshire Mental Health Trust

1 What is Depression?

Depression is a distressing and painful emotional problem. If you have depression you may be sad and tearful, lacking in energy, feeling guilty, and not able to experience pleasure or emotion in the way you normally would. You may be worrying excessively and feel anxious. This chapter describes what depression is, and introduces some of the terms and ideas used throughout this book. We explain how depression differs from other disorders and from 'normal' ups and downs in mood. (Skip to Chapters 2 and 3 if you want to understand the causes of depression.)

CASE STUDY: Tim

Tim's mother died just under a year ago, and he was recently made redundant, following a company reorganization. He now suffers from depression and has been signed off work by his family doctor. He feels very low and pessimistic about the future much of the time. Tim typically feels at his worst first thing in the morning, when he wakes up around 5am. He usually goes to bed at around 11.30pm, having had three or four glasses of wine to help him sleep. However, he often finds that his sleep is fitful. Even though he wakes up early, Tim usually stays in bed thinking about his problems and about why he can't pull himself together until midday, when he gets up to watch daytime television. Sometimes he spends some time on his computer playing games or surfing the Internet. Although his appetite is much smaller than normal, to break his boredom he goes to his local shop once a day and stocks up on sweets and snacks. He washes these down with several cups of tea or coffee throughout the day. Tim's friends phone him from time to time in the evenings, but he usually avoids their calls. Throughout the day he has thoughts like 'I'm a failure' and is constantly critical of himself. He broods on what he would have been doing at the office. When he thinks about seeing his friends or going out to do things he would usually enjoy he thinks 'I don't enjoy doing anything anyway, so what's the point', and has no enthusiasm for seeing people or developing any relationship. In fact, Tim feels so ashamed of his current state that he prefers to keep himself hidden from his friends, unless he has a 'good day' – which is rare –and then he makes a huge effort to seem like his usual self. However, he finds this very tiring, and his friends then assume that he is fine and that he's simply not interested in seeing them any more. The longer he is off work, the harder it is to get back into the employment market. He finds it painful to think about his mother's death and tries to avoid seeing his father, who finds his son's behavior odd.

CASE STUDY: Emma

Emma and her husband had been dating for about seven years before they got married. She soon got pregnant, and changed her role from running her own business, over which she had full control, to being a mother. She started to feel isolated and no longer in control. Her relationship with her husband started to deteriorate and they don't communicate well. Emma feels down and tired all the time. She lacks motivation and sleeps for about 12 hours a day, including a nap every afternoon. Her appetite is low and she has lost about 14 pounds in weight. She is very critical of her appearance and ability to function. She ruminates on her past and wishes she had never met her husband and that she could turn back five years in time. Emma views the future as bleak and has had suicidal ideas. She feels irritable and tearful, hurt and angry and thinks a lot about the past. She avoids a wide range of social and public situations, including going to the gym, which she used to enjoy. Emma's parents now come to the house every day to look after her young son. She has shut down and lives each day as it comes. She cannot enjoy her normal pleasures and her sleep is disturbed. She drinks ten or more cups of coffee a day. Emma believes that if she were given a gun or some barbiturates she could easily kill herself, but does not have the courage to act and wants to stay alive for her son. Her parents understand their daughter's difficulty but are getting more annoyed with her as they feel she could do more to take more responsibility for her life.

CASE STUDY: Jan

Jan is a 50-year-old married woman who lives with her husband. Her main problem is a conflict she had with her daughter-in-law, which has led to the loss of any relationship with her son and grandchildren. It was a silly argument about childcare in which she was a bit critical of her daughter-in-law. However, she feels she cannot apologize or try to resolve the breakdown in their communication. She feels down and tired. Her concentration is impaired. She has difficulty in getting to sleep and wakes several times at night. Her appetite is poor. Sometimes she is more irritable than usual and gets headaches easily. She feels tense and constantly worries.

When Jan thinks about her son and grandchildren, she tries to think of 'happy' thoughts related to them. She tries to avoid thinking of the loss in the relationship with her son and ruminates endlessly on trying to understand why her son doesn't sort things out. She tries to give reasons for this (for example, he has a weak personality). Jan avoids having photos of her son around the house as it makes her tearful. She blames herself for being a failure and thinks 'If only I hadn't said anything.' She throws herself into housework and keeps herself busy so she does not have time to think about her relationship with her son. The family tries to avoid discussing the loss and sadness. Jan worries about what others might say if they found out, or how she may never see her son and grandchildren again, or the effect of her worrying on her health, or how she cannot solve the problem with her daughter-in-law. She avoids conflict with everyone and has learnt to be a peacemaker but cannot make it up with her daughter-in-law. Everyone thinks she is coping but inside she is experiencing a lot of pain.

Throughout this book we'll be referring back to Tim, Emma and Jan to help illustrate the process of regaining direction in your life, and improving your mood using the research-proven techniques outlined in this book.

Are you depressed?

Everybody feels down from time to time, but the feeling usually passes fairly quickly and doesn't interfere too much with the way we live our lives. When most people say 'I'm depressed' they mean that they are feeling low or sad, or perhaps stressed, which are normal facets of human experience. However, when health professionals talk of depression, they are using the term in a different way. They are referring to a condition which is qualitatively different from the normal ups and downs of everyday life. This is the type of depression we will be discussing: it is more painful than a normal low, lasts longer and interferes with life in all sorts of ways. However, there is probably a link between normal sadness and depression, with no clear dividing lines.

Checklist of symptoms

So how do you know if you are experiencing depression or are just going through a period of feeling low? Depression can only be diagnosed by a health professional, but to meet the criteria for a diagnosis you will have been feeling *persistently down or lost your ability to enjoy your normal pleasures or interests for at least two weeks*. In addition, you will probably have at least two to four of the symptoms listed on page 4 persistently. Tick off how many of these symptoms of depression you've experienced in the past week. If you are diagnosed as having depression, when you set out to overcome it, return to the checklist to help monitor how your symptoms are progressing.

☐ Significant weight loss (not because of dieting) or weight gain

☐ A decrease or increase in appetite

☐ Difficulty sleeping, or sleeping excessively

☐ Feelings of agitation or irritability

☐ Tiredness or loss of energy

☐ Ideas of worthlessness, or excessive or inappropriate guilt

☐ Reduced ability to concentrate or pay attention

☐ Reduced self-esteem and self-confidence

☐ A bleak and pessimistic view of the future

☐ Suicidal thoughts or attempts

The symptoms should be enough to distress you or handicap your life. The lowered mood should vary little from day to day, and not usually change according to your circumstances. However, it's not unusual for people who have depression to find that their mood is worse in the morning. There is a lot of variation between one individual with depression and another, especially among adolescents. In some cases, anxiety and agitation may be more prominent than the depression, or masked by features such as irritability, excessive use of alcohol, or a preoccupation with your health.

Severity of depression

Depression is often classified according to whether it is mild, moderate or severe, depending on the degree of distress and handicap it is causing you. So a health professional who assesses you will want to know whether the way you feel affects your ability to work or study, or your enjoyment of your social life and relationships, and even whether it is sufficiently distressing to make you want to end your life. You can monitor the impact of depression and anxiety on the quality of your life by completing the scale in Chapter 5. If you do this before and after what you are doing to improve your mood, you will see what effect those strategies have had.

You will be diagnosed as having **mild depression** if you have at least two of the symptoms in the list above and you can generally cope with your everyday activities. **Moderate depression** is defined as having three (or more often four) of the symptoms in the list and social, work or domestic responsibilities as being a real struggle. **Severe depression** is characterized by at least four other symptoms from the list. In this case, you are very unlikely to be able to carry on with your normal activities or responsibilities, except to a very limited extent. To be clear, though, even mild depression is a very distressing experience to the person concerned.

About 50 per cent of the depression and anxiety in the community is mild. The recommended treatment for mild depression is different from the treatment for moderate or severe depression. For example, antidepressants are not recommended for mild depression. There is, however, a whole menu of effective treatments for depression to choose from, which we discuss in Chapter 4. Antidepressants are effective only for people with moderate to severe depression; they are discussed in Chapter 16.

The effects of depression

The best way of thinking about your depression is to divide the symptoms into the way you **think**, the way you **feel** and the way you **act**. Not everyone experiences the same symptoms – they partly depend on the severity of your problem and your culture. Some people (especially young people) may experience more irritability. Elderly people tend to experience more physical symptoms, such as feeling tired or constipated or having headaches.

Effect on thoughts

Negative thoughts

When you are depressed, you tend to think negatively about yourself, the situation you are in, what you have done in the past, and your future. You might believe that you are weak or a failure and that the future is hopeless. The trouble is that when your mood is low, perhaps as a response to difficulties in your life, then negative thoughts can seem very real and hard to dismiss.

Throughout this book we'll be emphasizing the importance of recognizing that thoughts about yourself and the future are just that – thoughts, not reality. Learning to accept these negative thoughts willingly as 'just thoughts' and not buying into them as true has been proved by numerous studies to be an important part of overcoming depression. You may well have very understandable reasons for thinking negatively, such as painful experiences in your early life, and it's important to be kind and compassionate toward yourself about this. However, no matter how understandable it is that negative views of yourself, the world, or other people may have arrived in your mind, we want to help you learn to distance yourself from such views and be sceptical of their 'truth' so you can more readily move forward in your life.

Self-criticism

When you feel depressed you might be self-critical and 'label' yourself as useless, stupid or a failure. More severely depressed people tend to view themselves as totally worthless, unlovable or even bad. You may frequently focus on past mistakes which seem to confirm your negative view of yourself. However, when you are depressed, thoughts become *fused* with reality and accepted as facts. As a consequence, you develop a pattern of thinking which is like holding a prejudice against yourself. You are then more likely to avoid challenges or situations in which you believe others will put you down. You will learn in this book to notice when you are thinking about yourself in this prejudiced way by prefacing it with 'I had a *thought* that I was a failure,' thus underlining that it's just your thought or a mental event and not reality.

Helplessness and hopelessness

When you are depressed you may think that you are helpless in solving problems or feel trapped. You might believe the future to be hopeless and even want to end your life as a way of escaping from your problems. In depression, believing the future to be hopeless becomes fused with reality and people with the condition think that things cannot get better or can only get worse.

It is quite common for people who are experiencing depression to have thoughts of suicide, without taking the further step of acting upon those thoughts, like Emma in the example above. However, if you feel very hopeless about the future and are planning ways to end your own life, seek help **as soon as possible**. There's every chance you could still use the advice in this book to overcome your depression, but you may very well need support and assistance from a health professional as well. See Chapter 9 on suicide and Appendix 2 for details of how to seek professional help.

When 'thinking solutions' are part of the problem – ruminations

People with depression often attempt ways to improve the way they feel but unfortunately the techniques may leave them feeling worse. The following examples are discussed in detail in Chapters 2 and 6.

- **Avoiding** thinking about the situation you are in. This might bring temporary relief, but results in problems being left unresolved or building up.

- **Controlling** your thoughts or suppressing them, which can mean they enter your mind more frequently. You are probably trying to 'put right' or make sense of past events by **ruminating** on them, perhaps mulling over them constantly. Unwittingly you are probably trying to solve problems that cannot be solved or analyse a question that cannot be answered. This usually consists of lots of 'why?' questions. An example is that of Jan asking why her son cannot help resolve the situation; others include asking yourself 'Why am I so depressed?' or 'Why did my partner leave me?' Another favourite is the 'If only . . .' fantasies, as in 'If only I had taken her advice', 'If only I looked better.' Alternatively, you may be constantly comparing yourself unfavourably with others and making judgements and criticizing yourself. Rumination invariably makes you feel worse as you never resolve the existing questions and may even generate new questions that cannot be answered. The process of worrying is a variation on the same theme, in which you try to solve non-existent problems. These usually take the form of 'What if . . .?' questions. Examples include 'What if my partner had an accident tonight?' and 'What if I have cancer?' Chapter 6 will help you to 'think about thinking' in more detail and to cope better with your mind's invitation to try to solve non-existent or insoluble problems.

Loss of interest and pleasure

A common symptom of depression is a lack of interest in engaging in usual activities such as work, family life, socializing, and hobbies. Even if you are trying to 'carry on as normal' you might find that you get much less pleasure from your activities than you usually would. Doctors and therapists call this loss of pleasure **anhedonia**. It can be particularly distressing when people find that they don't have the usual feelings of love and warmth toward partners or children. It's vital to remember that these are normal symptoms of depression and the good feelings will return as your mood improves.

Changes in memory and concentration

Another very common and frustrating symptom in depression is difficulty in concentrating. Again, this will improve as your mood lifts, so it's very important to be kind to yourself. It is also not unusual for a person's memory to be affected by depression, leading them to become more forgetful. Combined with difficulties concentrating, this can sometimes even lead sufferers to worry that they might have something wrong with their brain, but this is an entirely normal symptom of depression and may be related to being excessively self-focused and living in one's head.

One of the more unhelpful ways that human memory is affected when people are depressed is that they more readily remember negative memories, and have difficulty recalling positive experiences. Naturally this can lead you to think more negatively since you may draw conclusions from a biased set of memories. This memory bias is also a real drawback at a time in your life when you are faced with difficulties, since memories of how you've solved problems in the past will be harder to recall. People with depression have difficulty accessing their 'positive memory bank', which is a very good reason to be highly sceptical of any negative conclusions you draw about yourself and your future.

Images

Images refer to pictures that just pop into your mind. Pictures are said to be worth a thousand words and they often reflect your mood. If you are very anxious, you might have mental pictures of bad events happening to you in the future. For example, a severely depressed person might experience pictures of being in hell. Treating images as reality can create many problems and it is important to recognize that you are just experiencing a picture in your mind and not reality.

Attentional processes

When you are depressed, you usually become more self-focused on your thoughts and feelings. This tends to magnify your awareness of how you think and feel in your inner world and makes you more likely to assume that your view of events is reality.

This in turn interferes with your ability to make simple decisions, pay attention or concentrate on your normal tasks or what people around you are saying. You are likely to be less creative and less able to listen effectively. In social situations, it means that your ability to focus on what people are saying or how they are really acting towards you is impaired. It may make you feel more paranoid. Your view of the world now depends on your feelings and the chattering in your mind rather than on reality. This also has an effect on other people, as you appear uninterested in them. We will discuss some ways to help you refocus your attention on the external world in Chapter 6.

Common emotions in depression

Changeable feelings

Feelings of depression or irritability often fluctuate. It's common to feel more down in the mornings and improve during the day. You may even feel pretty okay in the evening, yet feel rotten again the next morning. However, for some people it's the other way round and they feel better in the morning. Just remember that variation in how you feel is a common feature of depression, although more severe depression tends to be worse in the mornings.

Feeling anxious

Depression and anxiety frequently coexist. Anxiety is usually triggered by a sense that you are under threat or in danger. The threat may be real or imagined and may be from the past (for example, a memory), present or future. When anxiety dominates the picture, there is a typical pattern of thinking and acting. You may overestimate the degree of danger to yourself or others. Your mind tends to think of all the possible disasters that could occur. This is called **catastrophizing**. You may underestimate your ability to cope and see yourself as being weak or helpless. Your mind will want to know for certain or have a guarantee that nothing bad will happen in the future. This leads to worrying about how to solve non-existent problems and to control as much of your environment as is possible, or to plan ahead to deal with all the possible problems that might arise. When anxiety is very bad, you may be very agitated. This, along with worry, can make it even more difficult to get to sleep.

Anxiety can produce a variety of physical sensations too, including feeling hot and sweaty, having a racing heart, feeling faint, wobbly or shaky, experiencing muscle tension (for example, headaches or chest tightness), having cold, clammy hands, difficulty in swallowing, jumpiness, and feeling sick, having stomach upsets or diarrhoea, to list a few. If such sensations are misinterpreted as being immediately dangerous (for example, 'my heart is racing too fast, I'll have a heart attack') then this can lead to a very intense feeling of anxiety called a **panic attack**. Other symptoms such as persistent headaches may make you fear a brain tumour, but as there is no immediate threat you will simply become increasingly anxious.

Focusing on physical sensations

Some people (especially elderly people and those from certain cultures) do not describe feeling depressed or anxious but focus more on physical symptoms (for example, feeling tired all the time and being preoccupied with aches and pains). This can develop into a picture of chronic fatigue as they begin to do less and less and spend their time monitoring a particular sensation or pain to see if it has improved or not. Friends and family may want to see them less as they become so self-focused.

If you have this tendency to focus on your physical sensations, you may, for example, want to hide from the light by closing the curtains and to cut yourself off from all possible noise. Unfortunately, this has the effect in the long term of making you more sensitive to light and sound as your body compensates. You will learn in this book that focusing on your bodily symptoms and trying to avoid light and noise invariably make you feel worse. Instead we will try to help you refocus on what matters to you in life and to pursue it despite unpleasant feelings and physical sensations.

Feeling guilty

Feeling guilty is common when you *think* you have done something bad or broken a moral standard in some way (for example, having 'sinned' by doing something wrong or failing to do something good). Your mind might tell you that that you have let someone down, hurt someone's feelings, or caused offence in some way.

One of the things you might feel guilty about is having depression, and its impact on other people in your life. For example, you might have a sense that others are suffering as a consequence of your depression as you are being less attentive, or irritable, or not fulfilling your usual commitments. When you feel guilty you might have thoughts that you could have avoided your sin or error, and that you absolutely should have done so. When you feel guilty and are depressed, your mind may overestimate your personal responsibility for a negative event and you could blame yourself excessively. Your mind will not consider mitigating factors or other people's responsibility. Because you assume so much responsibility for having done a 'bad' thing that you believe you absolutely should not have done, you will be very likely to condemn yourself as a 'bad person'. You might also then tend to assume that other people will think of you in the same way, and that you are likely to be punished in some way for your 'badness'.

Guilt can be a very painful emotion and therefore you might be inclined to try to escape from it by using distractions or alcohol. You might find that you make un-realistic promises, to other people and to yourself, that you'll 'never do it again', to relieve your guilty feelings. Guilt may lead you to try to punish yourself or to deprive yourself of something but also – paradoxically – to avoid responsibility for your actions and putting things right if you can. You might frequently seek forgiveness from others or try to escape from your feelings. Another common behavioral response to guilt is to blame other people so as to 'shift' responsibility.

You will learn in this book to preface your view of yourself such as being 'bad' as 'I had a *thought* that I was bad' to underline that it is not reality, it's *just a thought*. Even if you have done something which contravenes your own moral standards, it doesn't mean you are a bad person through and through, it just means you are human and fallible – the problem is your 'solution' of constantly punishing yourself. You can learn to focus on improving your relationship with others and (possibly by making amends) follow your valued directions in life.

Feeling hurt

People most often describe feeling hurt when their mind tells them that they have been treated unfairly or unjustly, or that they have been let down by someone impor-tant to them. This typically occurs when you have been rejected or criticized. These events may have actually happened, or it may be that your mind jumped to the con-clusion that they happened. When you feel hurt and low, your mind might be inclined to magnify the extent to which you have been treated badly and the degree to which someone's actions 'prove' that they don't care about you. You might also overlook other explanations for a person's behavior that would help you see it as less personal. If, for example, after the break-up of a relationship, you tell yourself 'I'm unlovable. I'll be alone for the rest of my life,' you may be hiding your hurt with anger: you demand in your mind that your ex-partner should have treated you fairly and you just don't deserve to be treated the way you have been.

One of the main ways you're likely to behave when you feel hurt is to sulk (yes, adults do it too!). This means that you may stop talking to the person who you feel has acted in an uncaring way, and expect them (presumably through telepathy!) to realize how upset you are and make amends. You might also use an indirect form of punishment or way of letting the other person know you feel upset without telling them directly. Giving the person the cold shoulder, ignoring them, attacking them about an unrelated matter are all examples of this. All these behaviors have an effect on other people, as they are likely to be defensive or get angry too.

It can be helpful to consider alternative explanations for the behavior which has upset you; it may not be directly related to you at all. There may be some other cause entirely. Alternatively, you may treat 'personalizing' thoughts as symptoms of depression, rather than facts, and allow them to pass through your mind – they are 'just thoughts' and you don't have to sort them out. When you are depressed and feeling hurt, your lack of communication and withdrawal has a significant effect on others and this book will emphasize the importance of communication and working to improve your relationships with others.

Feeling ashamed

Shame is an intense, negative emotion when your mind thinks you are 'flawed' or 'weak' and should not have broken a personal standard. Many people wrongly think that having depression is a personal weakness and feel very ashamed of it.

If you are feeling ashamed of being depressed it's likely that your mind is over-estimating how abnormal it is to suffer from depression and assuming that only weak or defective people get it. In fact, depression affects one in six people at some time in their life, and can affect all kinds of people from all walks of life. There's also a chance that you'll be overestimating how much others will disapprove of you if you reveal that you have been feeling depressed, and how long they will think about and remember it. Most people will know of someone who has suffered from depression, and of course many other people will have had it too. It may take a person suffering from depression many months or years to face up to their depression and seek help. For many people this is because they feel ashamed of the way they are feeling and behaving.

If you feel ashamed, you may withdraw from others, to prevent them knowing you have a problem. The more you isolate yourself, the more it tends to feed your thoughts or ruminations. You might also avoid eye contact with people, and this could lead them to believe you are not interested in them and so they might steer clear of you.

This can also mean that people with depression often don't discuss their problems with friends, family members, or even their partner. There are several consequences of this. First, not discussing your feelings means not getting the feedback that those thoughts about being weak are just thoughts, not facts. Second, it can increase a sense of isolation, which can contribute to a low mood. Third, it can lead to a lack of support that can be so helpful when combating depression, and people who care for you might criticize you for not seeking help or discussing your depression with them (not, it is important to remember, for having depression).

Another behavior pattern you might fall into as a consequence of your shame is criticizing others to save face. This can be a major problem when people around you want to help you and lift your mood. If you feel ashamed you might be overly critical of others in order to draw attention to their weaknesses. The problem is that you're doing this only because you feel badly about your own problem, and it does nothing to improve the situation.

If you are not seeking help for your depression largely because your mind considers you 'weak' for having it, you probably believe you have to hide from other people and keep your head down. Shame is a common issue for people with depression, though it shouldn't be because it's an extremely common problem, affecting huge numbers of people from all walks of life. You are not a failure, it's just your mind producing the thought you are a failure. People don't choose to be depressed. The design fault lies in being human – although animals too get depressed, and psychologists have suggested that depression may once have been a helpful state to conserve resources in times of hardship when we were more primitive! Nobody – not even psychiatrists and therapists – can be sure they won't become depressed. We hope you will accept yourself for having an emotional problem, and strive to overcome it by not avoiding the problem.

Feeling angry and irritable

Some people (especially younger men or adolescents of both sexes) may experience being frequently irritable, angry, moody or aggressive rather than low or sad. Anger is a complex emotion: it can be a way of avoiding another emotion or thought, such as feeling hurt or fearful. Being short-tempered is thus often a feature of depression and a key issue is being able to experience the thoughts and feeling that have been obscured by the anger.

When you feel angry, your mind may label the other person in a global manner (for example, 'he is a total bastard') and demand that they should have acted differently. This usually has an effect on others, who may either retaliate or bad-mouth you and keep well away from you. We hope that after using this book you will be able to develop compassion for others and recognize that even if someone does something bad they are not a total bastard through and through, and that you will be able to communicate how you would like that person to behave differently.

Effect on actions

The actions of a depressed person are those of avoidance, inactivity and missing out on opportunities or pleasurable events. You may feel like an animal hibernating. You may be:

- withdrawn from social or public situations or putting off invitations to go out
- not answering the phone
- distracting yourself and watching rubbish on television or on the Internet
- neglecting yourself and showering or bathing less often than normally
- harming yourself (for example, cutting or burning your skin) to numb yourself
- drinking excessively
- taking an overdose of drugs as a way of emotionally numbing yourself
- not planning for the future
- avoiding conflicts or dealing with problems
- compulsively buying goods that you do not need.

The ultimate escape may appear to be to end your life and we discuss this in Chapter 9. When you are very anxious, you also tend to avoid situations that could make you more anxious or panicky – for example, because of a fear of others rating you negatively. If you are very anxious that a panic attack might prevent you from escaping from a situation in which you could be physically harmed, you might end up avoiding public transport or crowds altogether. If you do find yourself in a feared situation, you may use **safety-seeking behaviors**. These are things you do to reduce the risk of a threat. For example, very socially anxious people may keep their heads down, maintain poor eye contact, say very little and monitor themselves excessively to reduce the risk of being rated negatively and rejected. Unfortunately, these behaviors tend to rebound: other people interpret such withdrawn manners as a lack of interest in them so they make no effort to be sociable. Invariably, socially anxious people end up feeling unpopular and rejected.

In this book, we return repeatedly to the idea of escape, avoidance of situations or people and inactivity as these are some of the most important factors in maintaining depressed and anxious moods. The best way of overcoming your symptoms is to act against the way you feel and to test out what your mind is telling you.

Effect on your body

Having depression does not affect only the mind; it can have effects on the body too. Some of the biological symptoms of depression may be associated with a biochemical imbalance, such as increases in the stress hormone, cortisol. They include the following.

- **Sleep disturbance:** Different types of sleep disturbance occur in depression and anxiety. Depression is often characterized by waking early in the morning and not being able to get back to sleep. Other people – especially those who are feeling anxious and worrying a lot – may have difficulty in getting to sleep and may not nod off until the early hours of the morning. Alternatively, you may be sleeping too much and going to bed as often as you can to avoid feeling the way you do. Chapter 12 looks at sleep problems and some solutions.

- **Eating problems:** Core symptoms of depression are loss of appetite, eating less or missing main meals, and weight loss. Alternatively, some people eat chaotically, comfort-eat, gorge on junk food and gain weight. This behavior is another form of numbing yourself emotionally. When you are very anxious, you tend to lose your appetite. We discuss overcoming nutritional chaos or self-neglect in Chapter 13.

- **Loss of interest in sex:** Diminished interest in sex and, for men, difficulties in maintaining an erection, may be one of the earliest symptoms of depression to occur and the last to go. Anxiety also interferes with sexual performance. We discuss overcoming sexual problems in depression in Chapter 14 and problems with medication and sexual activity in Chapter 16.

- **Low motivation:** Not being motivated to do anything is a core symptom of depression. It comes with frequently feeling tired during the day, slowing down or lacking in energy. We will discuss how to overcome these symptoms in Chapter 7.

Types of depression

Health professionals classify depression according to the pattern of symptoms. Apart from the diagnosis of bipolar disorder (see below), these classifications are not particularly helpful as there are more similarities than differences between them. However, your doctor or therapist may use them and so it is important to know what they mean. Some diagnoses such as bipolar disorder may have implications for treatment, so we shall include them for completeness. The various possible diagnoses include the following.

Bipolar disorder

Bipolar disorder (or manic depression) consists of recurrent episodes of both depression and mania, a state of extreme happiness, euphoria or irritability. It is usually associated with being grandiose and losing your normal inhibitions. You may feel you do not need any sleep and your thoughts are racing. You may be very talkative and feel very creative. You may take excessive risks or spend large amounts of money. **Hypomania** is a milder version of mania which is more manageable. It is also possible to have a mixed state of both mania and depression. Bipolar disorder is much less common than unipolar depression and there is probably a strong biological factor in its development. If you have bipolar disorder, this book will be helpful for the times when you feel depressed. We recommend that you also read *Overcoming Mood Swings* by Jan Scott.

Unipolar depression

Depression is often described in terms of whether it is a single episode or recurrent. If your depression is recurrent, i.e. repeated *without* episodes of mania, then it is termed **unipolar**.

Chronic depression and dysthymia

Dysthymia is a type of chronic depression that persists for at least two years. Overcoming dysthymia is more difficult as your habits may have become more deeply ingrained. This might mean having to persist more steadily and for longer at achieving changes in thinking and behavior patterns. One of the main problems with long-standing depression is that people can find it hard to imagine feeling better as they might not remember 'good' times as easily. Another obstacle is a fear of making things worse, for example the idea that it is safer to be pessimistic and play it safe than to run the risk of being disappointed if your mood lifts and then worsens. Beware of your depression trapping you with pessimism. If you have long-standing depression, it is important to realize that you are not alone. Many people in a similar situation have found that they have been able to improve their mood more often and for longer by working on aspects of their lifestyle, attitudes and behavior.

Psychotic depression

Psychotic means losing touch with reality. One example is auditory hallucinations (voices you can hear when there is no one around – telling you, for example, that you should die). Another example is delusions (abnormal beliefs not held by others – for example, you are convinced that you are the Devil or that you should be punished in hell). Fortunately, psychotic depression is rare and is likely to have had a strong biological influence. Needless to say, if you are experiencing any frightening symptoms of the sort we have described then you must seek help immediately. Despite being serious and perhaps scary, psychosis is very treatable and you will recover.

Postnatal depression

Postnatal depression (PND) is an episode of depression that develops some time in the aftermath of giving birth. It can occur in the context of an unwanted pregnancy or a baby that is abnormal. More often, though, the baby is much wanted, and the mother has been looking forward to the birth and the labour went well.

The symptoms of PND tend to be the same as those for 'ordinary' depression – for example, feeling down, irritable and tearful, lacking in appetite, losing your ability to enjoy life and worrying a lot. PND is very common and may be *partly* related to hormonal changes following birth. However, men can also suffer from it.

Many women are a bit tearful, lacking in confidence or enthusiasm, and have difficulty sleeping by about the third or fourth day after having a baby. This is extremely normal and is often referred to as the 'baby blues'. It soon passes after a week or so and does not count as postnatal depression. If, however, these feelings persist over the next month or come on later, then you may be suffering from PND. It is more likely to occur if you have had PND with a previous baby, have a partner who is unsupportive or with whom you do not have a stable relationship, and have other problems, such as your partner losing their job or housing problems. A rare and severe form of PND is when a mother loses touch with reality ('puerperal psychosis'), which occurs in about 1 in 500 births. It usually comes on within a few days of the birth. This is similar to psychotic depression as described on the previous page, but the mother may be deluded that her baby is evil, or may feel suicidal, and in very rare cases she may take the baby's life with her own. Puerperal psychosis is usually a serious condition which may necessitate intensive support or admission to a specialist mother and baby unit.

Seasonal affective disorder

Seasonal affective disorder (SAD) is a type of depression that recurs regularly in the winter months and continues until the spring. It is dependent on the amount of length of daylight you receive, and so the timing tends to vary according to how far away you are from the equator. The symptoms tend to be different from classical depression and are more akin to hibernating for the winter – for example, sleeping more, overeating and lethargy. Treatment options could include the use of special lights (phototherapy). This is discussed in more detail in *Winter Blues* by Norman Rosenthal.

Types of anxiety problems

There are also a number of different anxiety disorders – which we do not focus on in this book – but which frequently coexist with depression. In fact, one of the most common diagnoses is that of mixed anxiety and depression. We therefore describe the main anxiety disorders below, and point you in the direction of reliable sources of information.

Generalized anxiety disorder

Generalized anxiety disorder (GAD) is characterized by persistent worry that is difficult to control. However, people with GAD often describe themselves as 'being a worrier' all their life and seek help only when their condition has become severe and uncontrollable. For a diagnosis of GAD to be made, the anxiety should occur most of the time. In most cases, the content of the worries are most commonly about relationships or health. To fulfil the diagnosis you will need to experience three of the following symptoms most of the time:

- restlessness or feeling keyed up or on edge

- being easily fatigued

- difficulty concentrating or mind going blank

- irritability

- muscle tension (for example, headaches)

- sleep disturbance (difficulty falling or staying asleep, or restless, unsatisfying sleep).

GAD can also cause a number of physical symptoms and interfere with your ability to function normally. It is a very common problem, either on its own or in combination with depression. For more information see *Overcoming Anxiety* by Helen Kennerley.

Panic attacks and phobias

A panic attack is a sudden surge of intense anxiety. It makes you want to escape from the situation you are in, and peaks within ten minutes. It includes at least four of the following symptoms: palpitations or racing heart; sweating; shaking; shortness of breath or feelings of suffocation; feeling choked; experiencing chest pain or discomfort; feeling sick or having stomach pains; dizziness or light-headedness; hot flushes; a feeling of the world or you being unreal; and tingling sensations. If you experience these sensations and misinterpret them to mean you are about to die, lose control, 'go crazy', or have a heart attack, then you will feel more panicky, and this will lead to a vicious circle. Panic attacks may come out of the blue, without any warning or obvious reason. Others may occur in particular contexts, for example when travelling on a train. If you then avoid such situations, you can develop a **phobia**. Agoraphobia is a fear of having a panic attack, leading you to avoid a wide range of situations which are linked to panic from which you cannot escape easily. When it is bad, you can become housebound or go out only with a family member. Further information can be obtained by reading *Overcoming Panic* by Derrick Silove and Vijaya Manicavasagar. Depression and panic attacks or agoraphobia frequently coexist.

Social phobia

Social phobia consists of excessive anxiety in social or performance situations (where you may be scrutinized or judged by others). People with social phobia fear they will do or say something that will be humiliating or embarrassing. They may fear that other people will see them blush, sweat, tremble or otherwise look anxious. They try to avoid participating in meetings, talking to strangers or people in authority, eating or drinking in public, dating, or being the centre of attention. Social phobia is diagnosed when the social anxiety significantly interferes with your life and stops you doing things that you would otherwise like to do. When it persists and becomes chronic, it is often linked to low self-esteem and depression. Effective treatment of social phobia usually improves the depression, although some people will require treatment of depression in its own right. For more information read *Overcoming Social Anxiety and Shyness* by Gillian Butler.

Obsessive compulsive disorder

Obsessive compulsive disorder (OCD) consists of recurrent intrusive thoughts, images or urges which the person finds distressing. These typically include thoughts about contamination; harm (for example, that a gas explosion will occur); aggression or sexual thoughts; and a need for order. It is associated with avoidance of thoughts and situations that might trigger the obsession or compulsions. These are actions such as washing or checking which have to be repeated over and over again until you feel comfortable or certain that nothing bad will happen. Depression frequently occurs alongside OCD. It is usually secondary to the OCD, and if you no longer have OCD then your mood will tend to improve. However, occasionally depression is the main problem and you have OCD only when you are feeling depressed. For more details see our book *Overcoming Obsessive Compulsive Disorder*.

Body dysmorphic disorder

Body dysmorphic disorder (BDD) consists of a preoccupation with an aspect of your appearance or a minor defect that is either hardly noticeable to others or not really abnormal. It leads to severe distress and handicap, and is often associated with marked avoidance behavior, checking your appearance in reflective surfaces and constantly comparing your features with those of others. Some people affected by

BDD may pick their skin or seek cosmetic or dermatological procedures. As with OCD, depression is usually secondary to the BDD; if you no longer have BDD then your mood will tend to improve. Psychological treatments for BDD also involve overcoming depression using the principles in this book. We are currently working on a book on overcoming body image problems and BDD.

Post-traumatic stress disorder

Post-traumatic stress disorder (PTSD) is an anxiety disorder that people can develop after being affected by one or more traumatic events. They usually experience a combination of symptoms such as unwanted thoughts and memories of the trauma; flashbacks; nightmares; feelings of upset or irritability when reminded of the trauma; avoiding talking or thinking about the trauma or reminders of it; feeling emotionally numb or cut off from other people; loss of interest in activities that used to be enjoyable; difficulty sleeping; difficulty concentrating; being overly alert or vigilant; and feeling jumpy. For more information see *Overcoming Traumatic Stress* by Claudia Herbert and Ann Wetmore. Depression frequently coexists with PTSD and may need treatment in its own right using the principles in this book.

How common is depression?

Depression is one of the most common mental disorders, and at any moment affects between 5 and 10 per cent of individuals seen by family doctors. Two to three times as many people may have depressive symptoms but do not meet the full criteria for depression. Twice as many women as men are affected. Depressive disorders are the fourth most important cause of disability worldwide and they are expected to become the second most important cause by 2020. Depression occurs less commonly in children, but by the age of about 16 it is as common as it is in the adult population. The rates decrease slightly in elderly people but remain frequent. It can thus affect people of all ages, cultures and backgrounds.

Depression is the third most common reason for GP consultations, although many cases go unrecognized. This is because many people go their doctor with physical complaints (for example, feeling tired, not being able to sleep, headaches or back pain). They are not asked about, do not divulge to the doctor or do not experience symptoms of depression which are easy to recognize. Most people will feel better with treatment within about six months, whereas for a few people who refuse help, the natural history of depression can last more than two years. GAD is even more common than depression. However, as we pointed out earlier, people are less likely to seek help for this condition as many view themselves as 'just a worrier'. Left untreated, some forms of depression may persist for several years, or recur regularly at times of stress. With help and some action on your part, there's every chance you can overcome your depression.

Famous people who have had depression

Given how common depression is, it is not surprising that there are many dozens of famous people who have or have had depression. Actors, scientists, poets, artists, authors, professors, politicians, religious leaders, doctors, comedians, psychiatrists and therapists have all experienced depression. No human on the planet is completely guaranteed to avoid depression in the course of their life. However, following the principles in this book will help improve your odds dramatically. Here are some famous people who have suffered from depression:

Charles Dickens (author)

Winston Churchill (British prime minister)

John Cleese (comedian, actor, writer)

Stephen Fry (actor, writer)

Audrey Hepburn (actress)

Thelonious Monk (musician)

Vincent van Gogh (artist)

Isaac Newton (physicist)

Mark Twain (author)

Mary Shelley (author)

2 What Causes Depression?

This chapter summarizes what is known about the 'causes' of depression and what makes someone vulnerable to experiencing it. Although it can be important and useful to have *some* understanding of how you have come to develop an emotional problem, we do not want to encourage you to look endlessly for reasons or causes. Usually there are either obvious triggers to an episode of depression (for example, the break-up of a relationship or loss of a job) or vulnerability (for example, being abused as a child) or genetic inheritance from a family history of mental disorder.

When considering possible causes for your symptoms of depression, it is usually helpful to think of three groups of factors, those that:

- have made you vulnerable to developing symptoms (for example, childhood abuse, trauma, genetic inheritance, and unknown factors)

- have triggered your symptoms (such as recent life events)

- maintain your symptoms (the way you react, with particular patterns of behavior and thinking).

We will discuss the third factor – that is, the patterns that maintain your depression – in the following chapters. It is within your ability to change them, and doing so is the cornerstone of self-help and cognitive behavior therapy. In this chapter, we will examine the first two factors.

A psychological understanding of the development of your depression can help you to take a more sympathetic, compassionate view of yourself, and thus be more effective in your attempts to recover. However, we don't want you endlessly trying to 'get to the bottom of it all'. Exploring possible root causes ought to be a relatively brief process – when you fall down a hole, you don't need to know the exact route by which you arrived at the bottom in order to climb out again.

As we outlined in Chapter 1, there are different types of depression. Partly because of this, scientists, doctors and therapists do not fully understand what causes it. What we can safely say is that depression results from a person being vulnerable owing to a mixture of psychological and biological factors and life experiences since birth, and that often there are long-term difficulties that set it off. To complicate matters further, people with the same severity of symptoms on a rating scale may have a different pattern of symptoms and combination of causal factors. For example, a young woman with good family support and a happy childhood, but a strong family history of depression, may experience the same severity of depression on a rating scale as someone who was emotionally and sexually abused as a child and now has two small children to bring up on her own in appalling housing.

At one extreme, depression can occasionally be caused by a medical problem such as an underactive thyroid gland. At the other, factors such as long-term parental neglect and a deep sense of being unloved that has lasted from childhood may be important factors in a person's depression.

Although we will discuss different contributions that are relevant to depression, such as psychological and physical factors and life experiences, they all interact with each other. Imagine that the cause of depression is like a glass full of liquid. The components of the cocktail in the glass will be different for each person and they will also mix and interact in different ways. The point is that having depression is like having the glass full – it will just vary from one person to another according to how much of the glass is filled by different liquids.

A word of caution about 'causes'

Trying to work out the exact 'cause' of your own depression can be difficult. Spending too much time trying to work out 'reasons' may lead you to avoid other feelings and prevent you from trying to solve the real problem of not doing what you value in life. Some of the causes of your depression may be in the 'unknown' category, buried in many years of life experience and evolution. However, in most people, the factors that have contributed to depression are fairly straightforward. People who feel unlovable, rejected, alienated, bullied or pushed down are those who are vulnerable. However, even if a partner is, for example, critical and demanding, there will be other factors such as your temperament, genetic predisposition, the way you respond to your partner and how you subsequently cope which will determine whether you develop depression. If you respond by avoiding your difficulties and don't pursue your own valued directions in life, then your life will be less rewarding and further lower your mood.

What makes a person vulnerable to depression?

Depression seems to result from a person's vulnerability to it and the presence of a trigger. Vulnerability to depression could result from three issues: personality or psychological traits; physical conditions that include medical, biological and genetic causes; and life experiences. These factors are not clear-cut, and there is a certain amount of overlap between them.

Psychological factors

Certain aspects of your personality may make you more vulnerable to developing depression. For example, you may be a perfectionist and set unrealistic goals for yourself, or excessively shy and reserved, or very dramatic. Such traits, in combination with one or more triggers, can make you more vulnerable to depression. As pointed out earlier, there is a certain amount of intermixing of the factors: it is clear that some aspects of temperament are partly genetically determined.

Physical conditions

Genetic factors

Depression can sometimes run in families, with as yet unknown genetic factors. If a close relative has depression, you may be at increased risk of suffering it at some time in your life. However, bear in mind that depression occurs naturally in up to 10 per cent of the population so it is merely elevating a normal risk. It is complicated because someone may have experienced depression mainly because of difficult childhood experiences and not because of a gene that increases their vulnerability.

However, genes usually require a life experience or a context to 'switch on'. In different or better circumstances the person concerned might not develop depression at all. Life experiences might include adversity during childhood or adolescence, such as emotional neglect, bullying or sexual abuse.

Medical 'causes' of depression

Very few medical conditions aggravate or mimic depression. However, if your history suggests a possible medical cause or if you are not getting better with conventional treatments, it is important that such causes are investigated despite their relative rarity.

- **Thyroid problems:** Having an underactive thyroid (**hypothyroidism**) might lead to weight gain, forgetfulness, excessive tiredness, a hoarse voice, slow speech, constipation, feeling cold, hair loss, dry rough skin, irregular periods and infertility as well as symptoms of anxiety and depression. This condition is easily detected by a blood test for thyroid function and can be treated by a thyroid supplement. **Hyperthyroidism** (having an overactive thyroid) can mimic a state of anxiety, with excessive agitation and weight loss.

- **Vitamin B6 deficiency:** Vitamin B6 aids the production of chemicals in the brain and is therefore important for normal functioning. A deficiency of this vitamin can result in depression but it is rarely found in anyone who eats normally. It is more common if you neglect yourself and have a poor diet. The level of vitamin B6 in your blood can be tested; if it is found to be too low, you can be prescribed a supplement. In rare cases, depression can be a side-effect of oral contraceptives which may be linked to B6 deficiency.

- **Folic acid deficiency:** A deficiency of folic acid may result from a poor diet, excessive alcohol consumption, malabsorption in the gut or chronic diarrhoea. A deficiency can also occur during pregnancy or with the use of oral contraceptives or anticonvulsants. Symptoms of folate deficiency include depression, insomnia, loss of appetite, forgetfulness, irritability, fatigue and anxiety. Folic acid deficiency may be a contributing factor in some cases of depression and it is worth getting yourself checked for it if you are not getting better. It can be treated by a folic acid supplement.

- **Vitamin B12 deficiency:** A deficiency of Vitamin B12 could result in depression, but this is very rare and unusual with a normal diet. Treating with vitamin B12 can rapidly relieve depression.

- **Excessive alcohol and drug use:** Alcohol and recreational drugs can be important factors in causing depression, and we discuss this in more detail in Chapter 14.

- **Use of certain medications:** A prescribed drug for a medical condition (for example, an antimalarial drug) can, on rare occasions, cause depression. If you have any doubt, check on the product information leaflet that comes with the medication and always discuss it with your doctor before stopping medication.

Biological causes of depression

Some doctors believe that depression has a biological cause such as a 'defect' in brain chemicals or an illness in the brain, like migraine. This sort of explanation may reduce the stigma and blame attached to people who have depression by ignorant people who think that they should just 'pull themselves together'. However, biological factors alone do not fully explain the symptoms of depression, and the stigma is not necessarily reduced. Furthermore, such explanations don't place enough emphasis on the context of the depression and the variety of possible ways of coping with particular events.

Biological explanations for some types of depression are supported by research using brain scans which show decreased activity in the frontal lobes of the brain of people with depression compared to those of people without the condition. However, the activity in the brain tends to return to normal following therapy or medication. This suggests that the abnormal brain activity is a *consequence* of depression rather than a cause. (For example, a fast heart rate occurs in a panic attack but this is not the cause of the attack, it's a consequence of anxiety.) It also means that there is no permanent brain damage in most people with depression. However, there are some medical conditions, such as multiple sclerosis, which may make you more prone to developing depression, over and above the difficulties from a long-term disability, when biological factors are more relevant.

Chemical deficiency in the brain

Biological explanations focus on the role of chemicals such as serotonin and noradrenaline (norepinephrine) in depression. These chemicals are part of the nervous system and allow one nerve to communicate with another. Serotonin plays a part in many aspects of normal human functioning, including appetite, sexual desire and anxiety, so it is not unique to depression. An imbalance of serotonin is not therefore necessarily a cause of depression.

Medication that helps to enhance activity in nerves that use serotonin or noradrenaline (norepinephrine) can help depression and anxiety, and we shall look at such drugs in detail in Chapter 16. *However, just because drugs that help depression act on nerves that contain serotonin, it does not mean that there is a deficiency of serotonin in depression or anxiety*. This is like saying that if aspirin improves headaches then headaches are caused by a deficiency of aspirin. The changes in serotonin are likely to occur *as a consequence of your mind trying to switch off*. Drugs that address the imbalance in serotonin may help in depression (and anxiety disorders) by enhancing the function of serotonin nerve cells in the brain. If your mood improves or anxiety lessens, then it may help you to cope better and to face up to and deal constructively with any difficulties you may have. Furthermore, as there are different types of depression it is possible that some types have a stronger biological basis than others.

In summary, trying to unravel the biology of depression is complex, and statements that depression is *caused* by an imbalance of serotonin or other chemicals in the brain are simplistic nonsense. Unfortunately, many people have been peddled this theory by pharmaceutical companies and cannot see the wood for the trees.

Remember that any biological changes observed in the brain of a person with depression can be reversed by using either a psychological or a physical therapy. If a person overcomes their depression (by whatever method), the brain will switch off the biological changes that may occur *in reaction* to the depression and the system will return to normal. There is no permanent structural damage in most people who recover from depression, and the use of medication does not tell us anything about the cause of depression.

What can trigger depression?

Depression usually occurs as a very understandable response to specific events and in a particular context. Many of the triggers in depression are long-term difficulties which may drain you over time. The most common triggers for depression are:

- loss (for example, the death of a loved one, the break-up of a relationship, the loss of a job, ill-health, lost opportunities or a severe financial downturn). For some people, loss is very difficult.

- changes to your role in life (for example, moving job, children leaving home, increased responsibility and stress at work). These are particularly difficult when such changes occur without any choice.

- conflicts in a relationship (for example, with your partner or a family member). These are especially difficult when you may cope by subjugating your own needs and feel resentful that you are not being heard.

- a sense that things are missing from your life (for example, a relationship, children, or a job)

- failing an important exam, not achieving adequately at work and feeling ashamed about the consequences

- chronic physical illness or pain

- jetlag or anything that disrupts your sleep.

Sometimes depression seems to occur out of the blue, without any identifiable trigger or social factors. In this case there are probably more biological factors at work (especially in bipolar disorder). In this case you may be excessively critical about being depressed and coping by avoiding getting support from your friends and family.

Anxiety is usually triggered by a threat to your:

- health

- social standing

- finances

- relationships with loved ones.

People with anxiety tend to overestimate the degree of threat to themselves or underestimate their ability to cope with such threats. The key issue in all of these contexts is the meaning you attach to the event (or series of events) *and* the way you deal with them. You may also feel threatened by the experience of anxiety. You might misinterpret the sensations of anxiety (heart racing, feeling short of breath, dizzy) as evidence that you are going to have a heart attack, suffocate or collapse and die, and develop panic attacks. When anxiety or panic attacks becomes a long-term problem it becomes a major risk for developing depression.

Understanding the psychological causes of depression

We tend to assume that being normal is 'healthy' and that abnormality involves disease. This fits with most physical problems. Evolutionary psychologists reject our understanding of depression as an illness for most people and question whether being healthy is normal. Their analogy is that happiness for a dog or cat is easy. So long as it is given shelter, warmth, food and water, is in reasonable health and is given a bit of attention and play, then it will be happy. If humans are denied any of these, it is not difficult to understand why they are miserable. However, most of us have our basic needs met – we have shelter, are warm, have food and water, are physically healthy – and yet many of us are unhappy. Indeed, having all sorts of material comforts, or even being an extremely attractive millionaire with a loving partner, a high-status job and caring children, does not make people immune from depression. This seems puzzling, although animals that experience loss or defeat may also experience a type of depression.

Psychologists note that mental suffering is extremely common, so much so that it is almost part of the human condition. This fits with the Eastern or Buddhist philosophy that *life is suffering*. Such an approach views the problem as not being inside (like bad genes or faulty thinking) but on the outside. In other words, it's *normal* to feel sad when bad things happen or you have lost an important relationship.

This is not to say that there are no biological factors in depression (especially in bipolar disorder and severe depression). There are several types of depression and, even when there are strong biological influences, the way you react to your depression still influences the severity of the symptoms. For example, if you have a significant genetic component to your depression you may be ashamed and depressed about being depressed (a 'double whammy'). The way you respond by being withdrawn, inactive and ruminating on how awful you are for being depressed could determine the severity of your symptoms and speed of your recovery.

Even if you are recommended medication for depression and decide to take it, there is nothing to stop you improving your mood by using the approaches described in this book. This will involve developing a more compassionate and caring view of yourself, acting as if you truly believed you had nothing to be ashamed of, and doing more of the activities you are avoiding.

Another way of thinking about your mind is that it consists of a large number of modules, each crafted to do certain jobs. For example, there is a module for fear, another for memory, and so on. In some mental disorders, there may be damage to a module. In conditions like dementia, for instance, there may be damage to the module for memory. In other disorders, rather than having a disease or damage to the brain, certain modules are trying too hard or shutting down because there is an excessive load on the system. Depression can be regarded as a *failure in a system because it is overloaded and has shut down*. It is overloaded because of the way you try to escape from unpleasant thoughts and feelings, or control your feelings by ruminating about the past or worrying about all the bad things that could occur. A *normal* process in the brain is trying to fix unpleasant thoughts and feelings. It is coping the best way it can – waiting for bad feelings to go away before you decide you can cope. This process can be seen in abnormal brain scans and serotonin activity. In our opinion, these biological changes do not cause the depression but are more of a *reaction* to it – the consequence of the mind desperately trying to escape from and control the way you feel. This is not to say that the biology is not important as it becomes part of the process. For example, when you are stressed, your cortisol level goes up and over time this will impact on your serotonin. As your serotonin goes down, you may feel more tired and it affects your sleep and the next day this will affect your way of coping. Your body and your mind work together and one has an effect on another.

However, you can switch off these biological responses by acting against the way you feel and in ways that will lead to better feelings. We shall develop this psychological understanding of depression in the next chapter.

The assumption behind mental health problems is that we are a product of our genes and what we have learnt since we are born. The way we think and act is shaped by our experiences, though some people are more vulnerable to depression through greater biological risk or particular personality traits. Throughout this book we emphasize the importance of the context – lots of 'bad' events may occur, especially in childhood, from emotional and physical abuse and neglect and lack of boundaries. If we experienced unpleasant events when we were younger, we tend to avoid anything similar and anything which remind us of them when we are older. If you were criticized or not loved during childhood, it would not be surprising if you grew up believing yourself to be inadequate or worthless. You would also be adversely affected if you learnt from people in your family not to show your emotions or to express them in dramatic ways, or if you were punished inconsistently or not set any boundaries. Much of our development arises outside of our awareness and we are exposed to literally millions of moments of learning. It is scientifically impossible to unravel or organize them into a causal order. This is why therapies that promise to 'get to the bottom of it all' and discover the cause of your depression in childhood are often unhelpful. Such therapies may sometimes make things worse and encourage you to ruminate on the past.

If you have very low self-esteem and are very self-critical, you may justify your actions as a way of protecting yourself or even deserving it and making sure you are not hurt or not criticized by others. In this book, we will be examining if this really prevents bad things from happening or whether it makes it more difficult to achieve your valued directions in life.

Identifying your triggers and vulnerability

We have argued that the 'cause' of your depression is impossible to determine scientifically because it is a complex mix of your genes and millions of experiences since you were born. In this section, we will ask you to try and identify any obvious triggers or areas of vulnerability to developing depression.

We can describe this in terms of a flower. In the drawing, the roots of your flower represent the physical causes of vulnerability, such as your genes. Your psychological make-up and life experiences (the other two factors that lead to vulnerability) form the stem and leaves, and include your temperament and ways of coping with bad events in the past. Bad things that are happening now (that have triggered the depression) are shown by clouds and lightning (as it's never going to be all sunlight and warmth). If Tim (see Chapter 1) were to draw a flower, his would look like this.

Now try this exercise for yourself on a blank flower with its stem and roots (picture overleaf). Ignore the petals of your flower until page 66. You can consider the risk factors under the following headings.

Biological factors (your roots)

Are there any possible genetic or biological risks – for example, do you have a family history of mental disorder? Do you have a neurological condition like multiple sclerosis or chronic pain that puts you at greater risk of depression?

Psychological factors (your stem and leaves)

Are there aspects of your personality that make you vulnerable, such as low self-esteem, perfectionism, an anxious temperament, extremely high standards, or a significant degree of dependency on others? (These form part of the stem and leaves of your flower.)

Social context

Did you had any bad experiences like bullying or neglect when you were younger that might have made you more vulnerable and be less able now to cope well with stress? (These also form part of the stem and leaves.)

Have there been social or personal problems like the break-up of a relationship or a continuing conflict at work or with one of your children that have triggered your depression? Have there been any major losses? Have been there any major changes in your role in life? (These all form part of the clouds and thunder in the diagram with your flower.)

By writing down the factors that might make you vulnerable to depression and inserting labels on the roots, leaves and thunderstorms in your picture, you are building an understanding view of the development and 'history' behind your depression. This will help you to be less critical of yourself for having depression, and put your problems in context. There is a blank copy in Appendix 5.

I can't identify any factors in the cause of my depression

Don't worry if you can't identify some of the factors that make you vulnerable to developing depression. It can sometimes be difficult to be certain of the causes, especially if depression developed from a young age or if there is no family history

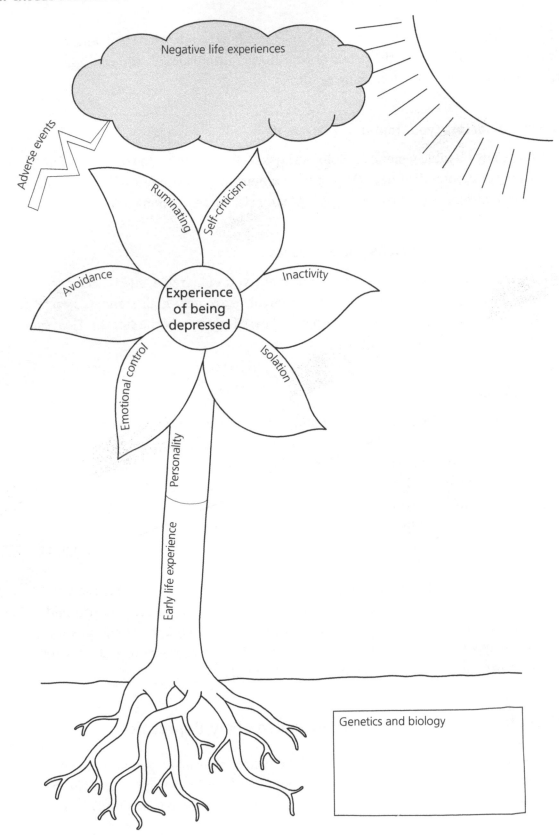

of a mental disorder. As yet, psychologists do not fully understand all the causes of depression. Constantly searching for a reason might seem like a good idea if you think that you need to find the reason before you can fix the problem. This approach usually works with physical problems: if you have a chest pain caused by a lack of oxygen to your heart from a blockage in an artery, then a doctor can do the right investigations to find the blockage and bypass the blocked artery with a graft. However, this approach does not work if you have an emotional problem, because the more you try to stop feeling depressed by searching for an elusive 'root cause' the more you focus on how bad you are feeling. You are likely to end up making yourself feel more hopeless as a result.

Inevitably, you will read or be told different things by different therapists or doctors. The more opinions you seek and the more books and websites you read, the more your doubts will increase. We mentioned earlier that some experts may emphasize the role of brain pathways and chemicals, while others may empathize with your childhood experiences. Change involves learning to tolerate uncertainty and accept that you will never know the 'exact' combination of factors that might be relevant for you. Some of the 'causes' are probably in the unknown category and, even if you knew the exact order of events, you probably can't do anything effective about them. Just say *no* to any therapy that offers to find the route you took into the hole. Insist on a proven psychological treatment for depression that helps you get out of your hole!

During therapy, memories you had before the onset of depression can sometimes be identified when you are doing things that you had previously strenuously avoided. For example, when a therapist was helping a woman to talk about past events that she had avoided and to do things that she found uncomfortable, it triggered memories of abuse when she was much younger which were clearly relevant to the development of her depression. Ever since then she had felt ashamed about the abuse, but these feelings had become generalized so that she not only avoided thinking about the trauma but also sidestepped many activities which had become associated with it. However, the relevance of the original trigger was identified only because of the emphasis on overcoming her avoidance behavior and getting back to a normal life. Once it was identified she could talk about the trauma, stop believing her self-attacking thoughts and develop a more compassionate attitude towards herself so that her mood improved.

3 A Psychological Understanding of Depression

As pointed out in Chapter 2, this book concentrates on looking at factors that keep your depression going – that is, those thinking and behavior patterns that reinforce your depression and maintain it.

Understanding how your depression is being maintained is the first step to overcoming it. In this chapter we will discuss a psychological understanding of depression, and discuss what keeps your problem going.

Thinking styles

Aaron T. Beck, the founder of cognitive therapy, and Albert Ellis, the founder of rational emotive behavior therapy, first described various styles of thinking that occur in depression and other disorders. These kinds of thoughts will run through anyone's mind some of the time, but when you're depressed you'll find they that tend to be more frequent and more extreme – and seem truer. We are not saying that they are wrong – in many ways they are extremely helpful in the right context. For example, the psychologist Paul Gilbert describes how if you were a primitive man or woman living in the savannah, you would need to think in black-and-white terms and to consider the worst if there's a chance of being attacked by a lion. In this case, it's better to be safe than sorry and to miss lunch – rather than be lunch. This sort of thinking is a normal part of stress. Unfortunately, the thinking styles that occur in depression are being triggered in the wrong context. Here are some of the styles of thinking that characterize depression.

- **Fortune telling**: Negative and pessimistic predictions about the future, for example, 'I'll never get over this'.

- **Mind reading**: Jumping to conclusions about what others are thinking of you, for example, 'She thinks I'm boring'.

- **Catastrophizing**: 'Worst case' thoughts and images that enter your mind, for example, concluding that something terrible has happened when a loved one is late coming home.

- **All-or-nothing-thinking**: Sometimes called 'black-or-white' thinking, this refers to thinking in extreme terms like 'I should do something perfectly or not bother at all'.

- **Demands**: Rigid rules you place on yourself and others: 'must', 'should', 'have to' and 'ought' are all words that often involve you making inflexible demands on yourself or others, which may not help you to accept and adapt to reality.

- **Personalizing**: Taking other people's actions too personally, or giving yourself too much responsibility for a negative event.

- **Mental filtering**: Focusing on the negative events in your life or your failings, and ignoring the positive elements or your positive attributes.

- **Disqualifying the positive**: Taking information that could be interpreted as positive and discounting or distorting it, for example 'That doesn't count', 'They're only saying something nice because they pity me'.

- **Emotional reasoning**: Thinking the way you feel indicates how things are in reality, for example, 'I feel I'm a hopeless case, therefore it's a fact'.

- **Fusion**: Similar to emotional reasoning. To 'buy into' thoughts (with their related memories and feeling) like they are facts i.e. 'fusing' thoughts with reality.

- **Labelling**: Globally putting yourself, others, or the world down, for example, 'I'm a failure', 'I'm useless', 'I'm worthless', 'He's so stupid', 'She's a horrible person', 'People are nasty', 'The world's a terrible place'.

- **Overgeneralizing**: Drawing a general conclusion from a specific event. 'Always' and 'never' statements are common, for example, when your car refuses to start and you think 'Nothing ever goes right for me'.

- **Frustration intolerance**: Telling yourself a difficult experience is 'unbearable', 'intolerable' or that you 'can't stand it'.

- **Awfulizing**: Labelling a 'bad' event as 'terrible', 'awful', or 'the end of the world'.

These thoughts are one interpretation of reality, and are extreme and unhelpful. They are really not worth engaging with and it is better to regard them as 'just thoughts' without buying into their message and believing them as facts. Thinking errors can be helpful to know since you can just label your style of thinking when they occur ('Oh yes, an excellent example of emotional reasoning').

New developments: Cognitive behavior therapy and variations

Much of this book is based upon the principles of behavioral activation (BA). It is also in keeping with acceptance and commitment therapy (ACT). These are newer developments within the family of cognitive behavior therapies (CBT). Research shows that BA is just as effective as traditional CBT for depression. There is some evidence that BA may be *more* effective for individuals with severe depression. BA was originally the 'B' in 'CBT', but it has now been developed as a therapy in its own right.

Putting aside 'internal' causes of depression

Behavioral activation differs from most psychological and psychiatric theories of depression in that it does not focus on an 'internal' cause for depression, such as your thoughts, beliefs, internal conflicts or a chemical problem in your brain. The assumption behind BA is that

the experience of depression is a consequence of avoiding or trying to control unpleasant thoughts, feelings and problems and trying to find reasons for the past or to solve unsolvable problems. The effect is that you become inactive and withdrawn from avoiding people and your normal activities. This in turn leads you to feel worse and you miss out on experiences in life that normally bring satisfaction or pleasure. Furthermore, the way you act has an effect on others and the environment around you that may make your depression worse.

Depression is thus highly understandable given the context you find yourself in (for example, a conflict in your relationship, the loss of your job). For many people, the appeal of this shift of emphasis from 'internal defects' (for example, lack of serotonin, faulty thinking) as an explanation for depression is that it helps them to feel less blamed or stigmatized for their problem. By focusing on the context and whether your reaction works in helping you to achieve what you want in life, it is a highly practical approach. Crucially, it's also a highly scientific perspective in the sense that the approach been scientifically proved to be effective and it rests on testable theories.

Why seeking reasons can make things worse

Given the relative lack of certainty about what the psychological and biological causes of depression are, it makes sense to focus on what makes the condition worse or better. Believing what your mind is telling you, for example, 'Why am I feeling this way?' or 'I'm depressed because of the way my husband treated me', or 'If only I'd found a way to make him different'; or 'Life is unfair, I don't deserve to be treated this way' may in fact be part of what keeps you depressed.

Depression can be made even worse when you buy into your thoughts (for example, comparing yourself to others and believing your mind telling you that you are a loser or weak), leading you to try to control or escape from them. Sometimes the methods you choose to avoid painful feelings (for example, becoming less active, avoiding people, drinking alcohol) can also serve to make depression worse. The approach we take in this book emphasizes that the willing embrace of uncomfortable thoughts and feelings, and acting in a way that is consistent with what's important to you, helps you achieve what you want in life.

Rumination and worry

Going over problems from the past asking yourself unanswerable questions (this is called, as we mentioned earlier, **ruminating**) and worrying about the future are important factors that keep depression going. As explained above, a critical difference between the approach we're outlining here and traditional CBT is that, rather than questioning the *content* of your negative thoughts (for example, 'I'm a failure') and *scheduling activities*, BD focuses on developing a different relationship with your thoughts and *doing the activities you are avoiding and following your valued directions in life*.

When your solutions are the problem

The American psychologist Steve Hayes has a useful way of describing people trying to cope with bad events that are not their fault. Imagine you're blindfolded and placed in a field with a toolbag. You're told that this is what life is all about and that your job is to run around this field, with the blindfold on. Now, what you don't know is that there are some deep holes in this field. So you start running around and are enjoying life. However, sooner or later you fall into a deep hole. You can't climb out and you can't find an escape route. So you feel inside your toolbag; maybe you can find something you can use to get you out. The only tool is a shovel. So what do you do? It's natural and highly understandable to start digging. It seems so obvious because you are stuck and can't get out. You try digging but soon you notice you're not getting out of your hole, so you try digging faster and faster; but you're still in the hole. So you try big shovelfuls, you try throwing the earth far away from you and so on, but you're still in the hole. Does this relate to your experience of trying to get out of your depression? You might be seeking help from this book or going to a therapist in the hope that you can find a bigger or better golden shovel to help you feel better. Well, you can't dig your way out. However, if you let go of the shovel, you can feel around to see whether there is anything else to help you out – a ladder, for example. Remember you are blindfolded and you won't be able to find the ladder or anything else until you *drop the shovel*. From the perspective of this book your shovel is analogous to the attempts you are making to control or escape from uncomfortable feelings, or trying to answer unanswerable questions and avoiding the activities that make you feel uncomfortable.

Looking at your actions compassionately

It is important to remember that, like falling down a hole in the example above, becoming depressed is completely understandable. Bad events do occur and to some people they occur more often than might seem fair. Yes, life is unfair, but it's not your fault you've fallen down the hole. You had the ability to get out, but before you started to read this book you did not know what to do and did what you did because it seemed natural. The way you are trying to cope makes perfect sense given the situation in which you find yourself. We are *not* saying that the situation is hopeless but, and this is very important, *your solutions of trying to avoid or control your thoughts, feelings and situations are not working*. All they do is make the situation worse and you get more depressed and stressed. If you can give up your current faulty solutions there is every hope for a long life which is meaningful to you, without depression. Remember, working out how you fell into your hole (or the route you took to get there) is not going to get you out of it. Some therapies unwittingly provide you with a better shovel.

Trying to dig is a natural response if you don't see an alternative – you are doing the best you can with the tools you have! Remember that only when you stop shovelling can you feel around for something to help you out. It is a leap of faith but, if you don't accept the uncertainty, it's guaranteed to get worse. The bottom line is that it's generally unhelpful to focus on finding reasons and working out how you ended up in a hole – you might justifiably do this once you are well and are out of your hole and living the life you want, as a way of trying to prevent a relapse and being more aware of 'holes'.

Identifying your problematic solutions (spot your shovel!)

So what is your 'digging'? This is what you are you doing to cope with your depression or stress. It generally falls into two broad areas: escaping from your thoughts, feelings and actions or excessive control of them. How does this occur? As mentioned earlier, a fundamental process is 'emotional reasoning' or 'thought fusion'. Thus if you *feel* worthless or believe the future to be hopeless, then that becomes your reality. Rating yourself as worthless and the future as being hopeless is treated as a fact like the sky being blue. Sometimes other people reinforce this tendency (for example, friends or relatives who say 'I'd be depressed too if I went through what you did'; or 'I'd want to figure things out in the same way'; 'You need rest to get over the way you feel whilst time will heal').

While you focus on your negativity, the process of fusing your thoughts and reality becomes missed as you totally buy into their content as facts. These thoughts are just mental chatter rather than objective evidence that everyone can agree with. We shall describe this in more detail in Chapter 6. The aim is to 'understand' these thoughts, not so you can question whether they are true or not, but to consider your relationship with your thoughts and how you react to them.

Escaping from difficult thoughts

If you have fused your thoughts with reality and believe them to be true, it's not surprising that you want to escape from them or from the feelings of depression. Thus, you may experience an emotional escape by feeling numb or uninterested. In order to escape unpleasant thoughts and feelings, you might start to:

- avoid activities and people that you normally enjoy and become more focused on yourself

- withdraw from friends or family

- use alcohol or drugs to numb your feelings

- ruminate about the past and try to work out reasons for the way you feel

- avoid calling friends because you think you may be criticized or rejected

- try to distract yourself with 'retail therapy' or going out all the time

- 'put your head in the sand' and pretend that the problems around you will go away if you ignore them.

- spend a lot of time watching TV or DVDs

- ignore the doorbell or telephone.

Such behaviors become habitual so you may not even be aware of why you are doing them. We will describe in Chapter 7 many ways of avoiding things, all of which serve the particular function of trying to escape from unpleasant thoughts and feelings. The problem is that the more depressed you become, the harder it is to focus on the events that you are trying to escape from in the first place. *Escaping is insidious as it feeds on itself and makes you more depressed and further and further away from the values that are important in your life.* You then miss out on normal positive experiences and pleasures that occur in everyday life.

In many ways escape is a natural response to try to avoid bad feelings. However, it also has consequences as you dig deeper into your hole and make yourself more depressed and stressed.

Thought suppression

One way of not facing unpleasant intrusive thoughts or images is to try to suppress them. This often occurs when people have experienced unpleasant events such as the death of a loved one or a trauma. However, suppressing intrusive thoughts also has an unintended consequence: it increases the frequency of the thoughts and makes you feel worse. It is very normal to have intrusive thoughts about distressing events as your mind is trying to sort out what's important to you. That's why suppressing such thoughts won't work, since your brain will keep putting them back into your mind to sort them out.

To understand how trying not to think of something makes it more intrusive, not less, try the following exercise. Close your eyes and try really hard not to think of a pink elephant for a minute – try and push any image of a pink elephant out of your mind. Every time you think of a pink elephant, try to get rid of it from your mind.

What did you notice? Most people find that when told not to think of a pink elephant, all they can think of is a pink elephant. Understanding the apparent upside-down way in which the human mind works is a key to understanding and overcoming depression. Very many people with this problem are caught in the trap of trying too hard to rid themselves of thoughts and doubts, and in fact this brings about the very opposite of what they want.

If you're still not convinced that trying to get rid of thoughts, images or doubts makes them worse, try a more 'real life' experiment. Spend one day dealing with your thoughts in the usual way, and record their frequency and the distress they cause you (step 1). Spend the next day trying twice as hard to get rid of your thoughts and record their frequency, and your distress. Try as hard as you can to suppress them (step 2). The following day go back to your usual way of dealing with your negative thoughts (step 1), and then the next day carry out step 2 again. Take a look at the results of your four-day experiment. What do you make of them? Most people discover that their thoughts become more frequent and more disturbing the harder they try to get rid of them. So, if you don't try hard to get rid of a thought or image you will find that it bothers you less. After all, a thought is intrusive only if you don't let it in and recognize it for what it is. Embrace such thoughts and fully accept them and carry them as part of you.

Learning theory

Learning theory can help to explain how your problems developed. It shows that the way you think and act has been reinforced by the environment. If as a child you had little affection from your parents and were bullied by your peers, then you might have learnt that you are unlovable or worthless. These beliefs then become linked with various other thoughts in your mind. You might compare yourself with others. Knowing where you stand in life means you will try to avoid any conflict with people 'above' you to reduce the risk of being rejected or humiliated. You might avoid or escape from people or situations where you think you could be criticized or rejected to prevent yourself from becoming hurt or depressed. The downside is that you become lonely and isolated in the real world and miss out on developing any normal relationships.

Trying to avoid or escape from difficult situations is a very natural response and often very helpful in the right situation. For example, it may be sensible to keep your distance from bullies, but at other times you may have to engage with them. It's all about finding the appropriate response for a given problem and not avoiding your thoughts and feelings about the bad events.

Another example is if, when you are feeling down and ruminating on why you feel the way you do, you escape by going to bed. Because you get away from the pain for a few hours you start believing that ruminating 'works'. So the next time you feel bad, you have trained yourself to ruminate or avoid activity and go to bed again. The problem is that this has consequences in the long term and makes you feel more depressed. You start to beat yourself up and tell yourself you are a failure; moreover, all the time spent in bed means that you miss out on what is important to you in life. It also prevents you from having any positive experiences, and strengthens the belief that you are a failure or unlovable as you are unable to test out your expectations. In Chapter 5, you'll learn how to do a functional analysis. This means having a good understanding of what is maintaining a particular pattern of thinking and behavior (usually escape, avoidance or control), and consequences, both short term (for example, feeling ashamed and depressed) and unintended (for example, irritation felt by others about your behavior and loneliness leading to further depression).

When problematic solutions seem to work

You may feel that digging your way out of a hole works because you are doing something with the tools you have and reducing bad thoughts and feelings. The activities are therefore learnt (like a habit) and can be difficult to break. So it is likely that you will avoid or escape from unpleasant situations in the future because such behavior has been 'reinforced', perhaps because it has been successful. We are not saying that this is wrong or bad; it just happens because human beings are like other animals and can train themselves to behave in a particular way. However, if you continue to cope by avoiding or escaping from unpleasant situations, the technique becomes unworkable for a number of reasons.

- Your solutions of avoidance and escape can make you feel worse and more depressed as you come to realize that they are not going to work and you begin to worry more about problems.

- Avoidance often prevents you from finding out whether something is true or not. For example, if you avoid discussing with a person why he appeared to ignore you, you will never find out if it was because he dislikes you or whether, for instance, he was not wearing his contact lenses or worrying about a problem of his own.

- Avoidance and escape has unintended consequences on your environment and the people around you. Your friends and family might stop trusting you and take on your responsibilities. This in turn could have an effect on your level of depression, in a vicious circle.

- You may miss out on meaningful events and opportunities that may be enjoyable and keep you interested in life. Avoidance stops you from doing what is important to you in your life – for example, you want to be a person whom your friends and family can turn to and be relied on for support, or want to be a good parent. When you can't do these things you will inevitably feel more depressed. You might spend more time focusing on yourself and beating yourself up and find that you cannot act in a way that is important to you. Your behavior then has an effect on your environment and others may be critical or unsupportive and you become more depressed, in a vicious circle.

Avoid avoidance, escape from escaping

Avoiding and escaping from bad feelings is like giving a bottle of vodka to a man who is stranded in a desert and dying of thirst. It might stop his thirst for short while but the alcohol will eventually dehydrate him further and he'll feel thirstier, or else he'll get drunk and give up looking for water and eventually die. The short-term solution becomes the problem.

Summary

In this book, you will learn the following.

1 You will recognize that symptoms of depression may be a message that something is wrong in your life from which you are escaping. This might be a problem in your relationship with your partner or a major change in your life that you are having difficulty adapting to. You will need to identify the problems you are avoiding and learn to tackle them step by step in the way a plumber would fix a leak. Look for guidance in Chapter 10 on problem-solving. However, problem-solving should be used only for problems that currently exist in your world or are very likely to occur (for example, you are being made redundant; or you are abused by your partner; or you are in conflict with your boss at work).

2 You will learn in Chapter 5 how to identify your ways of reacting to events and try to understand their function. The first step is to recognize how you are trying to control or escape from negative thoughts and feelings, or even situations, activities, people, or events that are associated with them (for example, going to the cinema, a conflict with your boss, or going to a party). In other words, anything that you might predict would be unpleasant. The function is usually to escape or control the way you are thinking or feeling. The aim here is to find activities that

will allow you to experience the feelings *better*. We we are not promising that you will be rid of unpleasant feelings or thoughts completely, because this is part of being human. However, they are likely to subside in intensity and frequency when you learn to see them for what they are – just mental events, and not a reflection of reality. You will also begin to have good feelings. Being alive means experiencing some suffering and having both negative and positive thoughts and feelings – *feeling sad about bad events is normal and healthy*. It's a natural reaction to loss, failing at something or adapting to change in your life. As has been stressed before, *depression occurs when you try to escape, avoid or control negative thoughts and feelings, and you become inactive and withdrawn so you miss out on the positive experiences in life and your actions has an effect on other people in the community.* When you learn to embrace these thoughts and feelings and see them as just mental events or neurons firing in your brain, and stop avoiding activities and people, you will be able to get back to your normal self and enjoy life again.

3 From Chapter 5 onwards, you will learn how to identify the situations you are avoiding or escaping from, or pleasurable, or satisfying activities that you have not tried before (or you have not done for a long time) as part of increasing your activity levels. The activities need to be varied and allow you to experience life. This is what you miss out on when you are depressed. Of course, the theory sounds easy and simple, but it may be difficult to implement. It may take an act of faith and repeated practice to break a habit.

4 You will also learn how to identify your values and what is important to you. Your activities therefore need to be consistent with your values. If, for example, you believe in being a good parent, you will set aside time to spend with your children. If you believe in helping your community and making it a better place to live in, or being a good saxophone player, then you will need to set aside time to act on these beliefs.

5 In Chapter 7 you will learn how to structure your day so that you incorporate your list of activities or problems to be solved and to monitor the effect of what you are doing.

4 Effective Treatments for Depression

This chapter discusses which approaches are effective for overcoming depression and which are not. We know this thanks to the enormous amount of research into depression that has been published. All over the world, experts in depression, including doctors, therapists and people who have experienced depression, have got together to review the evidence and produce treatment guidelines. Skip this chapter if you want to learn more about applying these guidelines.

In the UK, the body responsible for producing such guidelines is the National Institute of Health and Clinical Excellence (NICE), which is highly regarded through-out the world. The guidelines can be downloaded from their website (www.nice.org.uk). We have summarized its recommendations for the treatment of depression below. This will help you be more informed in any discussion with your doctor or therapist about any treatment that they may recommend. There is a particular emphasis in all guidelines on patient choice and on your experience with previous treatment. However, what treatment you have partly depends on the availability of therapists and local resources.

These guidelines are based on scientific evidence – that is, studies in which depressed patients are randomly selected to receive one or more different treat-ments. One group might be given a placebo or dummy treatment so that researchers can see to what extent the attention of a doctor or therapist and the passage of time affects the outcome. At the end of the study the researchers then re-test participants to see which treatments are more effective. The guidelines cannot cover every even-tuality, and if you are seeing a doctor or therapist, they will advise you as to what is best for you given the resources available. It isn't always obvious which treatment is most effective for a particular person. Sometimes you may have to try two or three different treatments before you find one which is effective for you. The core message is that there is a lot of evidence that *depression is treatable and you can get back to a normal life*.

Recommended treatments for mild depression

The following are all recommended approaches or treatments for mild to moderate depression in adults or adolescents. Mild depression was defined in Chapter 1.

'Watchful waiting'

Mild depression can get better by itself with no treatment, and your doctor or therapist may just keep an eye on you and provide some support for a couple of weeks. This is called 'watchful waiting'. If this applies to you, you should get a follow-up appointment to review your progress. Such an approach is very appropriate when the depression has been brief (for example, it has lasted only a few weeks). Mild depression often gets better by itself, especially if the symptoms are not too handicapping and there is support from your friends or relatives. It is usually precipitated by a crisis (for example, if your partner leaves you). If you have previously experienced depression or if after a few weeks your symptoms persist, then your doctor or therapist will want to recommend a more active treatment for your depression.

Counselling

There are many different types of counselling that might be offered to you for depression. Unfortunately, counselling is a minefield (even to health professionals), and there is no easy way of predicting what type of counselling you will receive. If you are referred to a counseller, your therapist may not even tell you what approach they use. Certain types of counselling (such as psychodynamic counselling) are in our opinion less helpful for most people with depression as they don't give sufficient hope. We believe they can unwittingly encourage you to ruminate by endlessly looking for reasons for why you are depressed. Counselling that is helpful for depression is focused on supporting you so that you can move on in your life and problem-solve rather than endlessly focus on past experiences. It should allow you to feel understood and supported in solving problems that you have been avoiding. For mild depression, the national guidelines recommend six to eight sessions of counselling over a period of ten to twelve weeks.

Problem-solving therapy

Problem-solving therapy is a psychological treatment that helps you to identify the problems to be solved and the steps you might take to try to solve them. It works well with solvable problems that you have been avoiding. Most people don't find it difficult to solve problems, but they may have been avoiding solving them for a variety of reasons. Problem-solving is generally used in CBT, although trying to 'fix' or control your internal world (such as your thoughts and feelings) the way you might fix a problem in the real world is not effective, and something different is needed. For mild depression, six to eight sessions of problem-solving therapy over a period of ten to twelve weeks is recommended in national guidelines. Further details of problem-solving therapy can be found in Chapter 10.

Cognitive behavior therapy and its variants

Cognitive behavior therapy (CBT) is a way of treating depression and it can be delivered in different formats such as individual or group therapy, and guided self-help by using a book or computerized CBT. It was founded by Aaron T. Beck, who revolutionized the psychological treatment of depression in the early 1970s. Beck rejected psychoanalytical theories and believed that depression was maintained by negative thinking and by being inactive. Components of CBT include activity scheduling, identifying negative thoughts and styles of thinking, and learning to distance one's self from negative thoughts and questioning their content so that alternatives can be tested out. This method of treating depression has been found to be as effective as antidepressant medication. Particular emphasis is laid on the 'homework' that you do to practise your skills between the sessions. A number of books can assist in guided self-help with traditional CBT; they include *Overcoming Depression, Feeling Good: The New Mood Therapy* and *Overcoming Depression and Low Mood* (see Appendix 4: Further Reading for details). A website that delivers CBT for preventing depression can be found at http://moodgym.anu.edu.au/

As mentioned in Chapter 2, the approach used in this book, behavioral activation (BA), is a development within the CBT family. It is a technical name for an approach that is described in a treatment manual for therapists. The 'B' in CBT has been developed and has become a treatment in its own right. The approach has been subjected to several tests that demonstrate its benefit. It is not generally included in national treatment guidelines because the results are still very new and it usually takes a few years – and a number of studies – for guidelines to be revised. In a large study published in 2006 that compared the effectiveness of BA, CBT and an antidepressant, all treatments were equally effective for mild to moderate depression. However, BA and the antidepressant were more effective than CBT for treating severe depression in the short term. BA is generally easier to learn than CBT and is certainly worth trying. This is the approach that is highlighted in Chapters 5–9. These chapters can also act as guided self-help when they are used with some input from a professional. If you find that the approach doesn't work for you, you can always return to classical CBT.

Exercise

Exercise can help improve mild depression. Taking up exercise is also part of changing your behavior. An exercise program usually consists of up to three sessions per week (lasting forty-five minutes) for at least ten weeks. For moderate to severe depression, exercise can be used as part of a program of activity in other areas. Exercise programs are discussed in more detail in Chapter 11.

St John's Wort

St John's Wort is a herb that can be an effective alternative to 'traditional' anti-depressant medication for mild depression. It can, however, interact with other medications. Chapter 15 looks at the effects of this herb in detail. We would not normally recommend St John's Wort as the only intervention for depression as it is important that you still tackle the problems or activities you are avoiding and aim to develop a life that's important to you. It is not recommended for adolescents with depression because not enough is known about its effectiveness or safety in young people.

Recommended treatments for moderate to severe depression

Medication

Moderate and severe depression were defined in Chapter 1. Medication and other physical treatments are usually recommended as an option in moderate to severe depression. You might have noticed that antidepressant medication was not recommended for mild depression. This is because antidepressant medication is no more effective than a dummy pill for mild depression. However, medication may nevertheless be recommended when your symptoms are mild but you experience recurrent depression and your doctor believes that your symptoms are likely to deteriorate (or if your symptoms have lasted for a long time). Antidepressants are prescribed to adolescents with depression only with great caution, and we discuss this in more detail in Chapter 16.

Combining medication with other treatments

In general, we do not recommend using medication alone because there is usually a higher rate of relapse when a person discontinues the medication than when it is combined with an evidence-based psychological therapy. However, given that there are different types of depression, a few people may do fine on medication alone and get back to a normal life with just that. The difficulty lies in identifying such individuals. Equally, there are some people who want medication (especially tranquillizers) to avoid having painful feelings. So think about the function of medication for you. If you have already tried more than one course of medication and are hoping that your doctor will come up with a drug that will get rid of your bad feelings, you are not really helping yourself. Trying to escape from a bad feeling is part of the problem and maintains your depressed mood. The main goal of medication is to *feel better* (that is, to stop feeling depressed), whereas the psychological approaches described in this book are generally geared to helping you have *better feelings* and do the things you value in life despite the way you feel. The two approaches may appear incompatible, but we have no evidence that one interferes with the other. If anything, some studies suggest that people with more severe depression may do better on a combination of medication and an evidence-based psychological treatment. It's worth being aware, though, that the goals of these different approaches seem to be slightly different and that more research is needed on the long-term effects of combining medication and effective psychological therapies in depression and how they interact. Unfortunately, mental disorder is complex and there are no easy answers. Whatever approach you take, make sure you monitor your progress with the rating scales in this book so you can decide (with your therapist or doctor) what is helping and whether to try something else.

Inequalities in funding for medication and psychological treatments

When you recover from your depression, please think seriously about campaigning on a political level for better access to evidence-based psychological treatments so that there is a real choice for everyone, and helping to raise funds for more research and psychological treatments into depression. For example, we need to know how effective BA is from just reading this book or whether there is a better result if you have a few sessions' support from a

continues on next page

mental health worker. Is combining BA and medication better than either treatment alone for severe depression in the long term? Working out which treatment is most cost-effective in treating depression can in itself be an expensive task. For example, medication seems a cheaper option in the short term, but if there is a high rate of relapse it can, in the long term, become a more expensive option as patients have to take the medication for many years. But proving this can be difficult and expensive because you need to study lots of patients. Pharmaceutical companies have plenty of money for research, whereas scientists who want to investigate psychological treatments have great difficulty in obtaining grants because the pot of money available is much smaller. This is partly related to the stigma of mental disorder – scientists studying cancer or heart diseases have a relatively easier time raising funds for research.

CBT and other therapies

The psychological treatments recommended for moderate to severe depression include CBT and **interpersonal therapy (IPT)**. It can be hard to find CBT in publicly funded medicine (like the NHS) in most parts of the world. Interpersonal therapy is another brief therapy that helps individuals concentrate on the link between symptoms and the losses and or conflicts in their life, the changes in their role and what is missing in their life, with the aim of focusing them on solving the problems they have been avoiding. Although it is recommended as an option, there are very few trained therapists delivering IPT compared to CBT. **Couple therapy** is another option if you have a regular partner and there are problems in your relationship (for example, your partner is excessively critical or jealous, and this feeds your depression). In these circumstances, we would normally recommend a cognitive behavioral approach within couple therapy with an emphasis on teaching both partners to communicate, negotiate and reciprocate with each other. This is outlined more in Michael Crowe's *Overcoming Relationship Problems* (see Appendix 4 for details).

For the psychological treatment of moderate to severe depression with CBT, you might be offered up to sixteen or twenty sessions over a period of six to nine months (although it could be longer or shorter depending on your need). For the earlier stages of severe depression, treatment sessions may be more frequent or you may be treated in hospital as an in-patient.

How long will it take me to recover?

This is very difficult to answer and depends on your circumstances. The amount of time taken to recover from depression partly depends on the context and the level of support. At one extreme, suppose you are a young person who has broken up with your partner. You have had a relatively happy childhood and have good support from your family or friends and no previous episodes of depression. In such a case, the outlook is very good and you are likely to improve by using the methods described in this book over the next month and be fully recovered within a few months. At the other extreme, let's suppose you have long-standing difficulties in your personality and in relationships. You may have been abused as a child and, if you do not have support from your family and friends, then it is likely to take much longer.

For many people, mild depression will go away of its own accord. However, no one can predict how long this will take – it could take a year or more, and the techniques described in this book can greatly speed up recovery. So using this book can be greatly beneficial to you.

Treatments that are not recommended for treating depression

All the approaches described above have good evidence to recommend them. Many others, from hypnotherapy to psychoanalysis, do not. Some of these approaches are well-meaning and the practitioners may passionately believe that they are providing effective treatments. Sometimes they are harmless, but at other times the opposite is true. As recently as 2005, a report from Russia described spanking with a cane as being an effective treatment for depression! Dr Sergei Speransk was reported as saying 'The treatment works. I'm not sadistic, at least not in the classical sense, but I do advocate caning.' He went on, 'At first they may not like it, but they come back for more.' He recommended thirty weekly sessions of sixty of the best, and insisted it was more effective if done by a member of the opposite sex. He claimed that caning works because it induces the body to produce it own opiates called endorphins, leading to euphoria. Unfortunately, vulnerable individuals are always subject to nonsense and pseudo-science.

Our advice is to use approaches that have research evidence and national guidelines to support them. If you decide to see a therapist, it's often a good idea to get a recommendation if you can, from friends or a GP. Check with the therapist about their level of expertise in treating depression, and make sure you feel they understand you well enough. The therapist should be able to give you a perspective on what they think is maintaining your depression and an idea of what to try out to help improve your mood and functioning. If this perspective and plan make sense to you, and fit your personal experience, then give it a try. There is more on selecting a therapist in Appendix 3.

5 How to Start Helping Yourself

This chapter is designed to help you measure and monitor your symptoms of depression, define your problems, set some goals for recovery and focus on the directions you'd like to take in life.

Rating the severity of your depression

Rating the severity of your symptoms at the start of your treatment and at regular intervals will help you to monitor your progress and assess whether what you are doing is effective or not. It's a good idea to use these scales even if you decide not to use any self-help or therapy or if you decide to take medication, as it is still important to monitor your progress so you can report back to the doctor and decide whether to try an alternative approach. The scale described below, the Hospital Anxiety and Depression scale, is a screening tool for depression and anxiety, and a way of monitoring your progress, and is reproduced by permission of Dr Phillip Snaith.

To use the scale, answer each question and add up your score for anxiety (in the left-hand column) and depression (in the right-hand column). You can summarize the scores on a chart (see Summary of HAD and Quality of Life Scores table in Appendix 5) so you can easily see the changes.

The Hospital Anxiety and Depression (HAD) scale

Please read each group of statements carefully, and then pick the one that comes closest to how you have been feeling in the past week. Write that number in the box. Don't take too long over your replies: your immediate reaction to each item will probably be more accurate than a long thought-out response.

                                                   Anxiety   **Depression**

1 *I feel tense or 'wound up':*

    0 Not at all
    1 Time to time, occasionally
    2 A lot of the time
    3 Most of the time

Anxiety   Depression

2 *I still enjoy the things I used to enjoy:*
   0 Definitely as much
   1 Not quite so much
   2 Only a little
   3 Hardly at all

3 *I get a sort of frightened feeling as if something awful is about to happen:*
   0 Not at all
   1 A little, but it doesn't worry me
   2 Yes, but not too badly
   3 Very definitely and quite badly

4 *I can laugh and see the funny side of things:*
   0 As much as I always could
   1 Not quite so much now
   2 Definitely not so much now
   3 Not at all

5 *Worrying thoughts go through my mind:*
   0 Only occasionally
   1 From time to time but not too often
   2 A lot of the time
   3 A great deal of the time

6 *I feel cheerful:*
   0 Most of the time
   1 Sometimes
   2 Not often
   3 Not at all

7 *I can sit at ease and feel relaxed:*
   0 Definitely
   1 Usually
   2 Not often
   3 Not at all

Anxiety   Depression

8 *I feel as if I have slowed down:*
0 Not at all
1 Sometimes
2 Very often
3 Nearly all the time

9 *I get a sort of frightened feeling like butterflies in the stomach:*
0 Not at all
1 Occasionally
2 Quite often
3 Very often

10 *I have lost interest in my appearance:*
0 I take just as much care as ever
1 I may not take quite as much care
2 I don't take so much care as I should
3 Definitely

11 *I feel restless, as if I have to be on the move:*
0 Very much indeed
1 Not very much
2 Quite a lot
3 Very much indeed

12 *I look forward with enjoyment to things:*
0 As much as I ever did
1 Rather less than I used to
2 Definitely less than I used to
3 Hardly at all

13 *I get sudden feelings of panic:*
0 Not at all
1 Not very often
2 Quite often
3 Very often indeed

Anxiety   Depression

14 *I can enjoy a good book, or radio or TV program:*
   0   Often
   1   Sometimes
   2   Not often
   3   Very seldom

Anxiety   Depression

TOTAL

If you score 9 or more on the depression sub-scale, you are probably experiencing depression. If you score 9 or more on the anxiety sub-scale, you are probably experiencing an anxiety disorder. Higher scores (15 or more on the depression sub-scale) may mean that a self-help book is not suitable for you, and you may need to seek additional professional help. There is a duplicate of this scale in Appendix 5.

Rate the impact of your problem on your life

The next step is to rate the impact of your problems on your everyday life. On the page opposite we have provided a Disability Ratings scale which asks you to rate the severity of your handicap in your life. There is also a duplicate of this scale in Appendix 5. Use the Summary of HAD and Quality of Life Scores table to record your results.

Defining your problem

Any attempt to solve a problem is only ever as good as the definition of what you think the problem is. This is especially important in overcoming depression because having a more accurate understanding of what the problem is forms a large part of recovery. For example, a faulty definition of the problem (for example, 'not knowing what made me depressed') leads to solutions that become the problem (for example, 'trying harder to find out what made me depressed'). Viewing other people

Disability Ratings

Please rate how far your problems have held you back in various areas of your life **in the past week**.
Circle the number that best describes how badly you were affected:

a Because of the problems, my *ability* to **work** or **study** or my role as a **homemaker** is affected.
(Note: please rate this even if you are not currently working; you are rating your *ability* to work or study):

b Because of the problems, my **home management** (e.g. cleaning, shopping, cooking, looking after my home or children, paying bills, etc.) is affected:

c Because of the problems, my **social life** activities (*with other people,* e.g. parties, pubs, outings, visits, dating, home entertainment, etc.) are affected:

d Because of the problems, my **private leisure** activities (*done alone,* e.g. reading, gardening, hobbies, walking alone, etc.) are affected:

e Because of the problems, my **general relationship with my partner** (e.g. affectionate feelings, number of arguments, enjoying activities together, etc.) is affected:

f Because of the problems, my **sexual relationship** (enjoyment of sex, frequency of sexual activity, etc.) is affected:

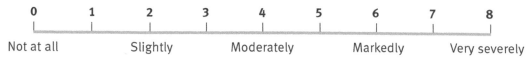

('my husband') or the situation you are in ('being alone') as the problem is also unhelpful as it does not describe your reaction. Problem definition has two distinct steps: first, a description of how you are thinking and feeling and the context in which you experience these feelings, and, next, the way you react to these experiences. You can define your problem and rate the severity of it on a simple scale between 0 and 10, where 0 is not a problem at all with no distress and fully able to function, and 10 is extreme distress and a virtual inability to function in any area of life. You can then monitor the severity of your problem at regular intervals to determine whether you are making progress. Tim, whose case history was set out in Chapter 1, defined his problems as below.

Problem list	Severity rating 0–10
1 Feeling life is pointless for the past year after the death of my mother, leading me to drink too much and avoid my friends.	8
2 Believing I am worthless after I was made redundant after 25 years with the same company, leading me to avoid friends or have any social life or get a new job.	7

In Tim's case, drinking too much was a form of emotional avoidance. Avoiding friends was a way of avoiding feeling depressed and having to discuss his redundancy or bereavement. Using the box opposite, try to make a list of all the problems you want to work on and put them in order of those that cause you the most handicap first to those that cause you the least handicap. You may decide later that some of these problems are related and you can combine them.

Problem list	Severity rating 0–10
1 _____	
_____	
_____	
2 _____	
_____	
_____	
3 _____	
_____	
_____	
4 _____	
_____	
_____	

Assessing the effect of thoughts and actions – functional analysis

What you do in your life has effects on you, other people and the world around you. To see how this works, you can do a *functional analysis*. You will need to do one regularly to work out whether what you are doing is helping you to achieve what you want in the long term. Doing such an analysis is usually straightforward, and Tim's history will give us an example.

We described in Chapter 3 how there are some activities that you do repeatedly because the immediate consequences tend to be rewarding and take away painful thoughts or feelings. So in the following table, 'A' stands for **Activating Event** (or trigger, also sometimes called an 'antecedent'). This describes the context in which the behavior or event occurs. It can be either a specific event (for example, being criticized by your boss or being ignored by a friend) or a general context (for example, your home being untidy). 'B' stands for **Behavior**. This is what you do or how you react (for example, escaping from the situation or trying to control feelings), and includes what you do in your head (for example, ruminating, worrying, or stopping thinking). 'C' stands for **Consequences**, or what happens next. There are often **immediate consequences** as there is some pay-off which makes the behavior more likely to occur again in the future (such as not having a bad feeling) and **unintended** (or usually long-term) **consequences** which cause many of the handicaps. Remember that unintended consequences affect not only yourself but also other people.

Tim's Functional Analysis

Activating event (the context of an event occurring)	*Sitting down on my bed to have a cigarette.*
Behavior (remember to include ruminating)	*Lie on bed.* *Ruminate.*
Consequences (immediate) which provide a payoff. What happens next? What effect does it have on your thoughts and feelings?	*Feel comfortable.*
Unintended consequences (in the long term) which cause handicap. What effect does it have on yourself and others? What effect does it have on the context?	*Feel more tired. Put off dealing with real problems. Ruminate more and become more self-focused and depressed. Others in my family become more critical.*

Now try your own functional analysis on a problem behavior or one that habitually occurs.

Functional Analysis

Activating event (situation or context of event)	
Behavior (what you do including ruminating, worrying and self-attacking)	
Consequences (immediate) which provide a payoff. What happens next? What effect does it have on your thoughts and feelings?	
Unintended consequences (in the long term) which cause handicap. What effect does it have on yourself and others?	

Identifying your own 'vicious flower'

It's important to identify the factors that maintain the problem and keep it going in a series of vicious circles that aggravate your experience of depression. One way of depicting this is to draw a 'vicious flower' diagram, in which the circling thoughts and responses that keep the depression going look like petals on a flower. Below and on the next two pages are vicious flower diagrams for the case histories of Tim, Emma and Jan from Chapter 1, showing how they respond.

Tim has identified a number of ways his depression is being maintained on his vicious flower. He puts his response in the clear box, and the effect in the shaded

Tim's vicious flower

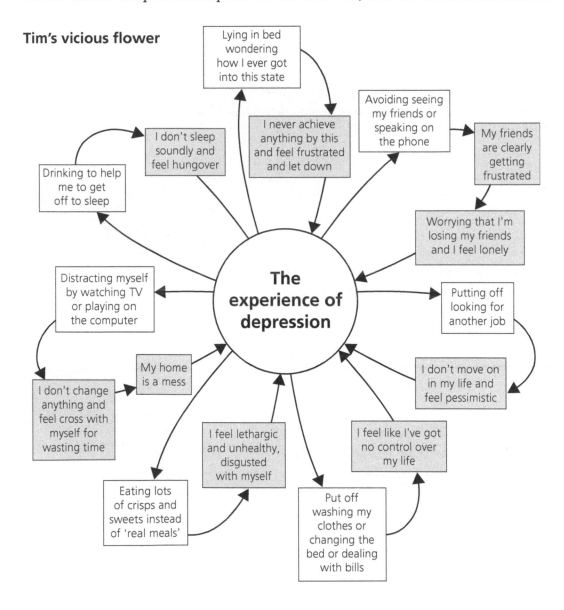

box. For example, he realizes that avoiding seeing his friends means not only does he feel more isolated, but in the long term this may put strain on some of his relationships, making his life less rewarding. He also notices that spending time in bed ruminating about his problem, especially about being treated poorly at work, really lowers his mood.

When you draw your own vicious flower the aim is to make connections between what you do (clear boxes) when you feel depressed and the *effect* (shaded boxes) of those responses. For example, spending more time in bed is a common response to feeling depressed and may feel more comfortable in the short term, but it will lead to you feeling more tired; sleeping poorly; missing out on activities that are normally satisfying or pleasurable; more difficulties with your friends or family, who may be critical or give up on you; and feeling more depressed.

Emma's vicious flower

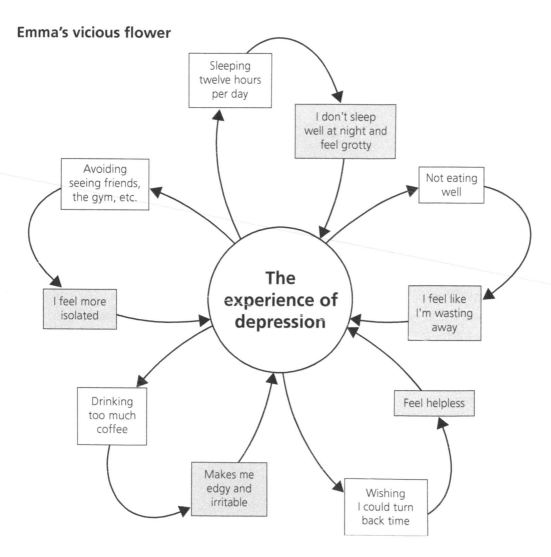

Jan's vicious flower

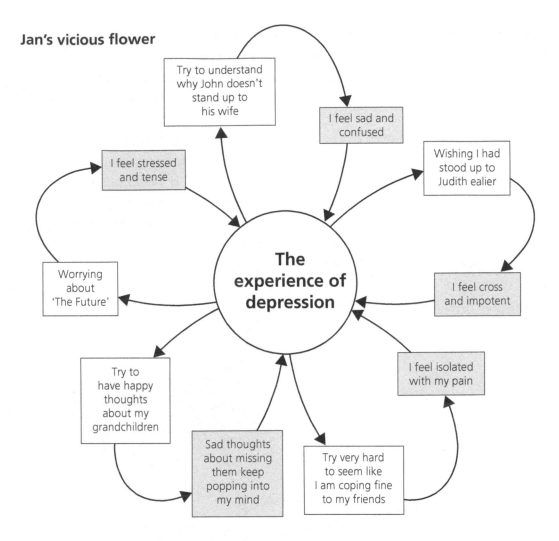

You can now fill in a vicious flower for your own problems (page 69). There is also a duplicate of the vicious flower in Appendix 5. Complete the boxes for your ruminating, avoidance and excessive behaviors, which all have an effect on your experience of depression. This in turn has an effect on others in your environment and reinforces your experience of depression. Once you have identified the maintaining factors in the vicious circles, then you will be able to make a plan as described in the next two chapters.

Try to consider the effect of your actions on your:

- mood
- living conditions
- sense of wellbeing
- body (for example, sleep, diet)
- relationships.

'Behavior' in this context includes 'mental behavior' such as ruminating ('If only . . .')
or worrying ('What if . . .'). Feel free to add more petals on your own flower.

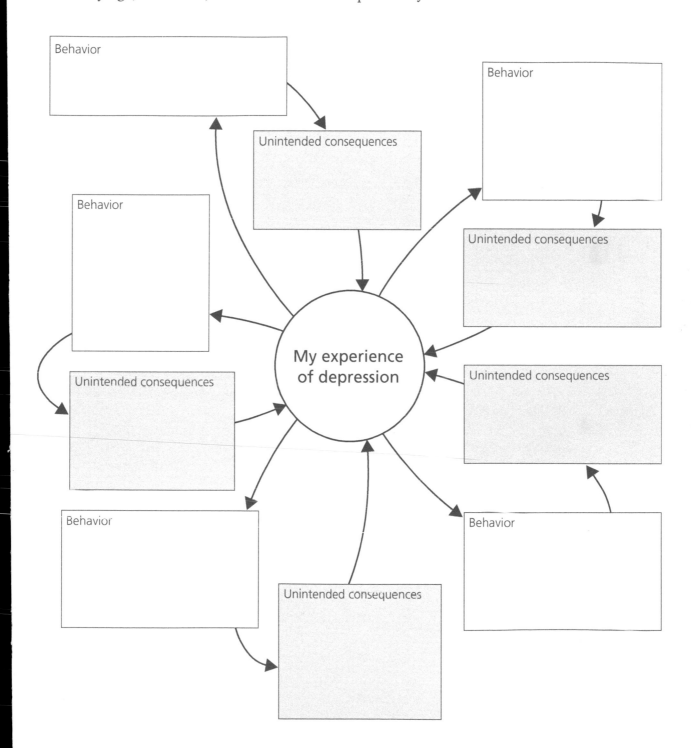

Behavior

Behavior

Unintended consequences

Behavior

Unintended consequences

Unintended consequences

My experience
of depression

Unintended consequences

Behavior

Behavior

Unintended consequences